That Old Devil Called God Again

The Scourge of Religion

That Old Devil Called God Again

The Scourge of Religion

Archbishop Jonathan Blake

CHRISTIAN
ALTERNATIVE

Winchester, UK
Washington, USA

First published by Christian Alternative Books, 2014
Christian Alternative Books is an imprint of John Hunt Publishing Ltd.,
Laurel House, Station Approach,
Alresford, Hants, SO24 9JH, UK
office1@jhpbooks.net
www.johnhuntpublishing.com
www.christian-alternative.com

For distributor details and how to order please visit the 'Ordering' section on our website.

ISBN: 978 1 78279 538 4

A CIP catalogue record for this book is available from the British Library.

Design: Stuart Davies

Printed in the USA by Edwards Brothers Malloy

CONTENTS

"The time has come to face our greatest challenge. We must find the courage to resign religion and our God-talk to history and begin to construct a new, international and all inclusive understanding of life that will unite the world"

Jade Goody's Bishop

Urges us not to fear the truth

** **Special additional features** **

Win Jade's eternal flame candlesticks

Read the inside story about her wedding and funeral

Plus non-religious words for baby namings, weddings and funerals.

For

H

J

P

S

A

N

D

G

About the book

The most controversial cleric of his generation publishes a scathing critique of Christianity, the great mistake made by Jesus and the scourge of religion.

He argues:

that the biblical God is immoral, cruel and abusive
that the Bible should not be given to children
that the virgin birth and resurrection stories are damaging
that Jesus made a big mistake in choosing crucifixion
that the Church is irredeemably corrupt
that worship has nothing to do with God
that the Mass is a means of control that has nothing to do with Jesus
that Christianity is a flawed human invention
that organised religion impedes our maturity and threatens our world

He writes:

'In a shocking example of racism, Jesus likened a desperate mother to a dog...'

'Jesus didn't die for us... his death served no good purpose.'

'Jesus was himself a victim of the irrational religious thinking that has blighted civilisation.'

'For Jesus, as for Islamic suicide killers, death held no terror.'

'The tears and heart break of partners and children appear to count for nothing in the face of the all consuming selfishness of religious zeal.'

'The story of Abraham being asked by God to sacrifice his son Isaac is among the most warped stories that could be read to children, yet schools and churches use it in their assemblies.'

It is a heinous concept that God would allow 'his own son' to be crucified and that his followers should drink his blood and eat his flesh.

'Worship is the most pretentious example of corporate delusional behaviour.'

'The evident facts are that there is no God as described by religion.'

Archbishop Blake has dedicated his life to the service of others and to the pursuit of truth and justice, continually railing against the status quo and challenging the stereotypes that contaminate society and morality.

He argues that Christianity poses a major stumbling block to our development and urges us to be brave enough to jettison our traditional beliefs and embrace a new and inclusive approach to the mystery of life that has greater integrity and is more truly spiritual.

About the Author

Jonathan Blake was born in 1956. He survived an air flight emergency when he was a child. Having graduated from Durham, he smuggled bibles and equipment to the Christian Communities behind the 'Iron Curtain'. He then embarked on an epic hitchhiking journey that saw him tear gassed in Teheran and seized by machine gun toting guards in Kabul, to work with Mother Theresa's Missionaries of Charity in Calcutta, India. He lived alongside the destitute in the Calcutta slums, barefoot and simply dressed, survived an attempt on his life and raised over £20,000 to support the poor, including the Howrah TB Hospital, and would carry sick children from the streets for treatment. He was ordained in 1981 and ministered as an Anglican cleric for the next 12 years.

During this time he slept on the streets to highlight the plight of the homeless, took Mass in rags to remember the poor, caused controversy by writing that workers at armaments' factories had 'blood on their hands', organised an inter-faith and international 'peace' bus for young people to Auschwitz and onto Moscow, travelled to Kenya, Australia, Pakistan and Switzerland to promote peace and justice and secured NHS funding for one of the first inter-faith hospital chapels.

In 1990 he wrote a biblical quotation on the Houses of Parliament, during a peaceful protest at the bombing of the Iraqi conscripts during the first Gulf War. He was arrested and charged and appealed to the High Court.

In 1994 he relinquished his office within the Church of England to pioneer the provision of Christian ministry independent of any denomination.

In the following six years he baptised over 1000 children in homes, gardens and community centres around the UK. He hit the headlines with a baptism on the top of Mount Snowdon and in a circus ring; with a wedding underwater and over the Internet.

He was the first cleric to advertise his willingness to provide marriage ceremonies for the LGBT community, which resulted in him performing hundreds across the UK and abroad.

In 1999 his book, *For God's Sake Don't Go To Church* was published, and he nailed his 95 Theses to the doors of Canterbury cathedral, was arrested but not charged.

In 2000 he co-founded the Society for Independent Christian Ministry and was consecrated a bishop. The following year he co-founded the Open Episcopal Church.

In 2001 he conducted the first gay wedding on prime time TV, on the Richard and Judy Show and subsequently sued Associated Newspapers for defamation.

He co-consecrated the first woman bishop for England in 2003.

He helped the homeless, providing accommodation for them, including using his own home. He took Holy Communion to the sex workers in Soho and food packages and hot-water bottles to the street dwellers.

In 2006 he was elected Presiding Archbishop of the Open Episcopal Church

In 2007 he consecrated the first woman bishop for Wales.

The Open Episcopal Church has grown under his archiepiscopate, attracting clergy from the Anglican Church and other denominations, ordaining gay and lesbian clergy and making the sacraments of baptism and communion available to all, even posting the consecrated elements of Holy Communion to people across the world.

In 2008 he was arrested for taking his children onto the roof for a school reading competition. He was released without charge when it was shown that he had used safety harnesses. However the police mistreatment he suffered led him to take out a private prosecution against the arresting officer for assault. He also founded a campaign group 'When No One's' Watching, to advise people about how to protect themselves against police malpractice. The group campaigns for all police work to be CCTV recorded. He also became an Independent Custody Visitor under the Mayor's Office for Policing and Crime, regularly inspecting the local police cells to check on the welfare of the detainees.

In 2009, he came to international attention when he was asked to conduct the wedding blessing of the celebrity star Jade Goody.

In 2012 he consecrated the first woman bishop for Scotland.

In 2012 and 2013 he was invited to Downing Street to meet the Prime Minister and invited separately to meet the Deputy Prime Minister, in recognition of his campaigning over two decades for equal marriage.

Previous Book
For God's Sake Don't Go To Church:
Published by John Hunt Publishing 1999
ISBN 0 85305 446 0

Part I

Chapter 1

Shock

(A warning – this chapter contains disturbing material)

The news is shocking.

Messed up.

We scan the papers, watch TV, survey history and are bombarded by appalling events.

Mayhem and bloodshed have been and are rife. Despotic regimes, irreconcilable differences and age-old disputes continue to soak the earth with blood. Geography, politics, history, culture, religion and economics are all players in the conflicts.

So many opposing sides pitted against one another and invariably a leader wreaking havoc.

Bashar Al-Assad

Muammar Gaddafi

Saddam Hussein

Slobodan Milosevic

Kim Yong Il

Idi Amin

Pol Pot

Mao Tse Tung

Adolf Hitler

Joseph Stalin… to name just a few…

All these male despots, wielding power over others for their own ends.

When Jeremy Bowen asked Gaddafi about the unrest and protests in Libya, he replied, "All my people love me". It is the delusion shared by most dictators.

Unbridled power, advantage and wealth corrupt.

Oceans of blood

In September 2013 Ban Ki-moon announced that the UN estimates that over 100,000 had been killed in Syria. We have seen the images of the bloated corpses of children pulled from the river in Aleppo, shot in the back of the head and watched the young writhing in pain after chemical attacks.

7000 are said to have died in Libya.

Tens of thousands slaughtered in Afghanistan.

Well over a hundred thousand in Iraq.

Over 500,000 in Rwanda…

I can have anything and do anything I want

It is reported that Gaddafi surrounded himself with female bodyguards. As well as expecting them to protect him, some have claimed they were raped and abused by him.

A 74-year-old Silvio Berlusconi boasted of sleeping with eight women in a night, offering to pay a 17-year-old £4 million for her silence about their relationship.

Osama Bin Laden was on his fifth marriage, the last being to a 17-year-old Yemeni woman, Amal, who allegedly he used as a human shield before being shot.

On December 7th, 2012 Nilofar Bibi was decapitated publicly by her brother in Kolkata, one of thousands of 'honour killings' around the world.

During the same month a physiotherapy student was gang-raped on a Delhi bus, and later died of her injuries. A spiritual guru, Asaram Bapu said the student was as guilty as her rapists.

The treatment of women around the world has been and remains shocking. The persistent features are their oppression and domination by men, who think they have the right to do to them whatever they choose.

In Kenya, in 2013, a 16-year-old, returning from her grand-father's funeral was raped by 6 men and thrown down a well. Her back broke during the fall. The assailants were arrested, kept overnight and then asked to cut the grass in front of the police station as their punishment, before being released.

No one weaker is off limits, not even a child

In 2010/11 over 23,000 children were sexually abused in England and Wales.

We have been incredulous at the extent of the abuse perpetrated by Jimmy Savile, a 'devout Catholic'.

Every week, at least one child is killed in the UK at the hands of another person.

Kristy Bamu's death in 2011 is a chilling example.

At 15, his sister and her boyfriend subjected him to a staggering act of depravity and cruelty over a four-day assault. He was beaten with a metal bar, which was then thrust into his mouth. He was struck in the face with a hammer knocking out his teeth. A pair of pliers was used to pull off part of his ear.

He was deprived of food and sleep. In the end he begged to be allowed to die.

On Christmas day he was put into a bath, doused with freezing water and drowned.

All this, because he had wet his pants and they believed he was a witch.

In Saudi Arabia, in 2013, a five-year-old girl, Fayhan al-Ghamdi , was raped, tortured and beaten to death by her cleric father who 'doubted her virginity' and who later was due to be released, after having paid 'blood-money'.

Severed heads

Parents fear for their children in Uganda.

Tepenensi found her six-year-old grandson, Stephen, decapitated in 2011.

Some believe that the sacrifice of a child brings a person wealth and good health.

The UK based charity, the Jubilee Campaign, claim that there are over 900 cases of child sacrifice that have not been investigated by police.

Pills of baby remains

South Korean officials have seized powdered human baby flesh in capsule form. 17,000 such pills were discovered in 2011.

In China, the baby corpses are dried in microwaves, pummelled and mixed with herbs. They are marketed as a miracle cure for all ailments and as stamina boosters.

There is speculation that the corpses come from China's one baby policy that leads to approximately 13 million abortions a year, as well as from the notorious 'dying rooms' where babies that exceed the quota are left.

Football, hopscotch and suicide games

Abdual Samat was 13 when he had explosives strapped to his body and was driven to Kandahar to detonate them. Fortunately childhood fears and tears prevented an atrocity.

Nothing prevented a fourteen-year-old suicide bomber in 2012 killing himself and 6 others near Kabul's NATO headquarters.

Gul Khan, a 10-year-old run away explained that his father had sent him to be trained as a bomber.

You can find on YouTube a video showing children playing or being trained to carry out a suicide mission.

A varied modern diet – including human flesh

In 2012 Rudy Eugene was discovered eating the face of a homeless man in Miami.

In Maryland Alex Kinyua admitted eating the heart and brains of his room-mate.

Mao Sugiyama served his severed genitals topped with button mushrooms and parsley to a group of diners in Japan for £150 a plate.

In 2011 Dennis Storm and Valerio Zeno underwent surgery to remove a part of their bottom and abdomen respectively. On a Dutch TV show, a celebrity chef cooked the flesh and the two presenters ate it at a candlelit dinner.

Our impression?

Stunned. Incredulity perhaps as we try and absorb these events?

What sounds feel appropriate for us to use in response? What words and images spring to mind that we can rely upon to express our view accurately?

Perhaps indistinct infant-like sounds alone are sufficient for us initially. We make undefined exhalations of air at the horror and insanity. We shake our heads in disbelief.

Then our mature enquiry begins, why and how could all this have come about? In the silence we ponder what has caused, influenced and led to this rottenness and devastation?

"Hey – Don't despair – We have the answers"

The 'speakers' who say these words are bold and insistent. Usually they greet us with smiles and warmth and the promise that they hold the key to make sense of the madness we have witnessed and will be able to point us to a better future.

We have to be intrigued. Often they come bearing a book or leaflets. They may knock at our door or confront us in the street. We may hear them on the radio or TV or from a pulpit. Let's hear their presentation, but we must be on our guard against being swayed by sweet words, corrupted by wild promises or conned simply by a well-honed sales pitch.

The speakers begin.

"We want to introduce you to the one who can sort out all this mess and chaos.

Our leader.

He's male.

His name is God.

He is a king and has a kingdom and he counts us as his subjects.

He governs us and creates our laws.

When we make mistakes, we can beg for forgiveness and he pardons us.

He is the most knowledgeable, powerful, wisest and richest ruler of all time.

He wants us to love him and worship him constantly.

He wants to rule everyone and everywhere.

He set about achieving this many generations ago by having a son.

He found a young virgin to have his child.

He was her 'heavenly' father, so you can dismiss those who claim that this was incest.

He is the God and king of the world, older than time itself and so you can reject too those who claim that he raped her and abused her. It is true that she was a young teenager and really had no choice in the matter – but kings traditionally have been able to do anything.

Further, God had a good reason.

He planned to have his son executed, to send him on a suicide mission in order to rescue the world. Actually it was to settle a bargain with the devil. "You murder my child as long as you let everyone else go free".

What generosity of spirit.

God decided that the sacrifice of his son would bring life and health to all.

The good news doesn't end there. Believers are able to eat his son too. His body and blood are distributed every day across the world by his followers.

Soon they may be offering him in capsule form…

Would you consider becoming a believer, a follower?

If so God assures you of a place in heaven, a hotline for prayer and his constant companionship and unconditional love…

that is... on the condition...

...you give your life to him first, and acknowledge his sovereignty over you and worship him night and day."

Gasps and silence

"Please" We begin to protest with a confused confidence. "You are not being serious, surely?"

"What you have described is perverted and disturbing. You haven't told others about this, have you?"

"Yes. For centuries these beliefs have been taught, to adults and children alike. They underpin 'Christian civilisation and culture'. They are the reason why...

"Why what... why male despots wreak havoc, why suicide bombers are the scourge of the world, why women and children are sexually, physically and psychologically abused, why children are being sacrificed and murdered and why cannibalism is on the increase."

The bald presentation the speakers have made is repulsive. However, it is the basic Christian message.

Normally it is decorated with familiar fudges, frills and follies. We recall Easter eggs and 'meek and mild' Nativity scenes and a smiling Jesus who is hugging children.

When it's stripped of its spin and we hear it bald and bare it is shockingly unpalatable. We are compelled to take a penetrating and fresh look at this religious narrative that has underpinned our lives and traditions.

Part II

Chapter 2

Tough Talk about Jesus

We must inspect the Christian beliefs that were imprinted onto our minds in childhood and have been with us ever since. We are obliged to examine the beliefs that may have contributed to a contamination and corruption of our lives and thinking as well as that of society. We are impelled to expose the dogmas that have had the power to impede our ability to evolve progressively and ethically.

Straight talking

Jesus wasn't a Christian and it wasn't his custom to go to a religious building.

The time he did, those inside threw him out and threatened to kill him.

He refused to be cowed by religion, by dogma or by ritual and raged against those who tried to trap others.

It was religious people who were responsible for his murder.

The great faith robbery

So why have we allowed religious people to steal his image and his message and allowed his 'followers' to pervert his legacy?

The Papacy, the Vatican, Lambeth Palace and the many denominations are not the true successors to Jesus and do not reflect his message.

Church buildings have extracted spirituality from people's homes and hearts and have made it a commodity.

Priests and ministers of religion have sought to control it, designing how Jesus is viewed and filtering those who have access to him.

We need to burst the dam walls of that control and liberate the facts.

The real Jesus

I have no interest in the plastic, manipulated and processed Jesus of Christianity.

I am intrigued by the complexity of the real Jesus.

The precocious 12-year-old Jesus ran away from his parents to pursue his hunger for knowledge.

The adult Jesus was so tormented by his desire to be rich and powerful, to be an exhibitionist and to plan a public religious stunt that he fled for a time into the desert to sort out this wayward thinking and decide a clear direction for his life.

He was an unusual man.

He found God at work in criminals and sex workers.

He was grateful for a prostitute's massage.

He said it was correct for hungry people to raid religious buildings and eat the bread they found there, even if it had been consecrated or reserved for God.

He made mistakes and had things to learn:

He was chauvinistic and rude to Martha.

He ruined the livelihood of a pig farmer, killing all his livestock.

In a shocking example of racism, he likened a desperate mother to a dog, because she came from another race.

He spoke bluntly; calling people he disliked 'hypocrites', 'disguised chambers of death', 'blind men' and 'snakes'.

He was willing to heal a member of the equivalent of Al Qaeda.

He told us to love the equivalent of the Taliban, Saddam Hussein and Colonel Gadaffi.

He criminally damaged the possessions of a group he regarded as 'rogue' traders, smashing up their goods and overturning their stalls.

He beat and whipped them, assaulted and wounded them.

He was a passionate unpredictable eccentric, an idealist and a radical.

Jesus' nightmares

Jesus had no intention of triggering the vast Christian empire that exists today. He showed little patience with the religious organisations of his own day and gave his life campaigning against them.

His night terrors were concerned with the mess human beings were making of their lives compounded by their religious observance.

He took every opportunity to try and defuse religion, render safe the spiritual cluster bombs that clerics had scattered and protect people from the tyranny of those who claimed to speak for God.

Initially the authorities tolerated his reformist rhetoric and his controversial slant on traditional religious understanding. It excited and enthused his followers and those who attended his rallies, but didn't provoke any revolutionary sentiments.

Alarm grew when his passion intensified and his criticisms became more personal and politically ambiguous.

It seemed that his exposure to a growing popularity began to alter his thinking. Often the adulation of others and undue attention creates a distorting influence. The one at the centre feels a weight of expectation and is pressurised to keep on producing material to maintain the crowd's interest and satisfy their commitment.

His attack on the religious leaders, his violence in the temple, his talk of revolution and war, his claim that he had come to bring division and fire upon the earth and his instruction to his followers to buy swords might have whipped up greater support but it gave the authorities little option but to become involved.

On the night of his arrest Jesus struggled with competing thoughts. Traditionally these have been presented as the battle between his own fear of martyrdom and his belief that this was God's will for him.

I suggest that Jesus experienced a very different battle. One waged between his desire to be martyred, as the logical end of his teaching and thinking, as the traditional religious choice of the fervent believer and as the ultimate public religious stunt about which he had battled in the desert, set against his worry that this would be a selfish, exhibitionist and egotistical choice.

He found his supporters asleep and urged them to pray to try and avoid being tempted as he had been.

He had succumbed to the alluring theory that choosing self-destruction indicates the ultimate devotion. The temptation he had resisted as a younger man had returned to snatch his life and having thrown himself to his death, he would find no angels coming to his rescue. The incentive Satan had dangled before him proved to be the ultimate lie coming from the prince of lies.

Selfish Jesus

Pilate tried repeatedly to have him released, but Jesus refused to co-operate. His replies to simple questions appeared designed to irritate. His silences were provocative.

He confounded Pilate's honest desire to find one way or another to free him.

Throughout history religious zealots have exposed themselves to excruciating physical agonies in pursuit of their belief. Jesus was to be no exception.

The Roman authorities meted out inhumane punishments routinely and were responsible for heinous acts of torture and murder. Pilate's reluctance to commit Jesus to this end was unusual. He sensed, as did his wife, the unusual holiness and grace within the man, but was faced with his religious obduracy.

Instead of Jesus using his intellect and skill with words to extricate himself from those who had conspired together for his death, he deliberately and actively invited it. He wanted to be martyred.

The warning signs

The seeds of religious extremism are often hard to discern. They are tiny seemingly innocent pockets of thought, which begin to take root and grow.

Jesus at first believed:

that God favoured the poor and the weak;

that the rich would find it hard to find God;

that the last would be first;

that you should live simply and worship God;

Then his thinking developed:

that you should invite someone who has attacked you to strike you again;

that you should maim yourself rather than tolerate temptation;

that you should love your enemies;

Then it evolved further:

that you should bless those who curse you;

that you should not be afraid of murderers;

that true belief results in you being insulted, flogged and killed;

Terrorism, martyrdom and sacrifice

We are used to the image of Jesus dying on the cross being portrayed as an act of selfless love.

We are told that it fulfilled God's will and formed part of a divine plan to save us.

*H*owever, such views have been challenged by the appalling acts of suicide bombers, which have become the scourge of the world.

Arguing that suicide bombers are different is not as credible as it may at first seem.

The argument that Jesus chose his own death but did not kill others is undermined by the deaths of all those who have felt inspired to follow his example.

The ultimate sacrifice, honoured by us all, involves a person being willing to sacrifice their life in the defence and protection of another from some evil. There are ample examples of heroic individuals across the world, from every faith and culture, whose names are forever hallowed, for their selfless service of others in pursuit of that which is good.

But looking closely at the experience of Jesus, removed from all the hype, does not permit us to place him in this category.

He chose to die as an expression of his religious fervour and his belief that this world was but a transitory staging post on the way to paradise. For Jesus, as for Islamic suicide killers, death held no terror. It was but a doorway to life, over which the religious and state authorities had no control and so different rules applied.

He could have chosen to answer Pilate's questions with wisdom and courtesy and achieved his release. Then he could have continued his teaching and his works of compassion. The people needed a wise spokesperson, who would not have been cowed by authority and who could have championed their causes, struggled to secure justice for them and improved their living conditions.

It was easier by far and an inferior choice to relinquish the grit of the everyday for the glorious but phantom rewards of heaven.

A deadly example

The cost borne by those that followed Jesus has been high. He must bear a responsibility for all those who have died subsequently, not to protect others, but following his example, out of a misguided religious fervour that led them to believe their lives were expendable in this world.

So many have broken the hearts of their families and friends and have denuded the world of their unique resource and individual spirits, out of a false belief that they were dying for Jesus. Even the most personal and intimate bonds are destroyed callously in martyrdom by the one holding the erroneous belief that they are heaven bound.

The tears and heartbreak of partners and children seem to count for nothing in the face of the all-consuming selfishness of religious zeal.

However, as we know the zealot rarely stops at self-sacrifice.

Jesus bears a responsibility also for all those who have been slaughtered and tortured at the hands of his followers, who have been willing to use violence and intimidation to enforce the Christian message.

Christian discipleship expressed itself at first by a person being willing to suffer passively, but then it went on to inspire many to die wielding the sword and worse against those who they regarded as unbelievers.

Decapitation, murder and torture have all been committed 'in Jesus' name' soaking the world in blood.

Jesus had shown life to be cheap and merely a passing moment in this world. Eternal reality lay beyond and true believers, eager to be assured of their place in that paradisiacal future were inspired by Jesus to surrender everything to that end.

Far from affirming life, its sanctity and unique status, Jesus had dealt a body blow to our existence, the repercussions and deleterious effects of which are still being felt today.

Jesus, the victim... of religion

However, Jesus was himself a victim of the irrational religious thinking that has blighted civilisation.

The separation of the material and the spiritual and the concept that this world is different from the next, inject a deadly disincentive to cherish our lives and the world around us.

Jesus was as susceptible to these influences as we all are. He was exposed to the persuasive religious sentiments that we ought to sit loose to this world, to be assured of our place in the next. Further that we ought to carry out instructions from beyond this world, even those to damage ourselves and others, because this world is transitory and subject to the control and the will of an ultimate divine authority.

There was nothing and no one to prevent Jesus' slide into radicalism and to a belief in martyrdom. He followed a well-trodden path and failed to appreciate that he would strengthen the precedent and be the cause of countless others choosing to go to their deaths with their sights fixed on paradise.

How much more useful would have been his legacy had he chosen not to perish and instead had halted the floodwaters of martyrdom. If he had fleshed out for us the precious and inviolable sanctity of life.

Does that mean that Jesus didn't die for us?

The traditional dogmas surrounding the crucifixion have been discredited.

The ideas that God had to do a bargain with the devil, that a ransom had to be paid or a sacrifice offered, that Jesus could be punished for our sin, that his obedience to God could mend and reconcile our waywardness, that death was defeated in a cosmic battle, that his blood satisfied an ancient debt, that God was empathising with our suffering, that his death became a mythical and mystical symbol of human suffering… they are all ridiculous to a modern eye.

No, Jesus didn't die for us.

His death served no good purpose.

It would have been better if he had not caused such suffering to his family and friends and had not placed them in such compromising positions.

If he had achieved clarity of thought and had mustered strength of spirit he could have perceived that martyrdom arising from religious fervour was a selfish option that denied and destroyed the sanctity of life. He would have conquered the allurement of death and its persuasive power. He would have exposed the trickery of egotism and exhibitionism masquerading as apparent self-sacrifice and he would have established the more meritorious principle of a holy life that was woven within the complexities of the everyday.

His legacy would have been the greater as he continued to practice a faith based on love and integrity and as he modelled an inclusive approach to community.

The crucifixion was his biggest mistake.

Chapter 3

Tough Talk about the Christian God

Updating and re-branding

God language is covered in cobwebs. It's from another time, culture and worldview. It has little connection with our lives and understanding. It represents a world of kings, servants, obedience, begging and rigid thinking.

In contrast, our society has leapt forward in its knowledge, perceptions and communications.

The following ideas, contained in the Bible are objectionable:

That God,

has a gender;

ordered revenge attacks;

required genocide;

commanded the murder of women and children;

supports capital punishment;

sanctions acts of rape;

impregnated a teenage woman;

appeared on the earth as a man called Jesus.

Modern thinking rejects the tenets,

that Jesus was both God and Man;

that he provides the only way to God;

that his follower's alone are God's chosen people who will live forever.

We must consider a complete and fresh appraisal of all these religious claims. The dilemma is whether anything meaningful is left once the upgrade process is complete.

Is there a place for God anymore?

What does the word 'God' mean?

In different languages, it is a different word altogether? Kami,

Jee, Duw, Allah, Dievs, Guuti, Bog, Isten, Olloh…

The truth is no one knows anything about what 'the entity' is to which these random sounds point. Saying the sound doesn't conjure up a specific image, not even one connected to a category like a car or a table. Instead every person will have his or her own image, perhaps entirely disconnected from other people's or not even known to themselves.

The images that the particular word evokes, which represent this 'entity' for us, are the collection of our assumptions, prejudices and cultural conditioning. The word is a screen onto which we project our thinking. Across the world, every person will fill hers or his differently.

However, there is an important difference. While we can agree that the word car relates to a recognisable object, the words/sounds for God we are using and the accompanying images tell us only about our thinking and have nothing to do with that to which they actually point.

We have no objective information about 'God'.

The significance of our words about 'God' lies in what they tel*l* us about *o*urselves.

Every society can be judged by its religion, which is the composite of its moral quest, codified in story, belief and dogma.

Every individual can be judged by his or her beliefs and the images they harbour of their divine.

So far, the judgements that must be made are bleak.

The very beginning

The question that tantalises us is when, where and how did it all begin. The ancient religious stories and poems, of which Adam and Eve is one, are quaint and intriguing, but one can't invite an enlightened modern thinker to believe they are accurate accounts.

No one knows how creation began. It remains a mystery. Science continues to uncover mind-expanding details about the early events, but the original question presses persuasively.

However much information emerges, the prior conundrum remains, of how something can emerge from nothing.

It is tempting to develop a tenet of belief – that God is the creative source and the beginning of all things. However, it is dishonest. We have no evidence for this and philosophically it poses insuperable difficulties.

The suddenly appearing God

We understand the movement from simplicity to complexity. The stages of human development provide a vivid illustration. Evolution charts the course from basic life forms to the multitudinous species at large today. Every year new research programmes and scientific discoveries enable even more intricate technological, biological and medical advances to be made.

Consider an adult human being, a computer, a space rocket, a magnetic resonance imaging machine. They have not just appeared. They are the result of hundreds of thousands of years of development.

It is nonsensical to suggest that a super-being, we describe as God, can just suddenly exist.

It is disturbing that people have become so dependent upon religion that they could find any comfort in such a belief. They are tantalised and overcome by the mystery of creation and their origins but find instant calm in being told that a being called God appeared one day and made the world.

Awe

Instead we must abide in the enormity and complexity of the universe. The questions that overwhelm us must immerse us in amazement and awe.

At times, meditating on what we do know about our existence, tugs us into an all consuming stillness, a shock and a breathless incredulity. It is impossible for us to comprehend the information. We are silenced by it.

For instance, in our galaxy, the sun is just one of hundreds of billions of stars. The number of galaxies cannot be counted, but in the observable universe alone there may be more than 170 billion. The Messier 91 galaxy is the brightest we can see by telescope and is 12 million light years away. Travel on another 34 billion light years and you come upon the edge of the universe. And beyond that...

We fret about today and tomorrow, but our planet existed for billions of years before we were born...

Terror

Such facts can provoke fear. The mind begins to fuse and shut down. People are tempted to comfort themselves by introducing a belief that God designed it all to make such immensity manageable and such anonymity personal. At a superficial level religion appears to do the trick, but it is an illusion. The truth is we are faced always with mystery.

In time, it may be that we can quantify and tame the mystery with knowledge and understanding.

It is possible that we will unc*ov*er evidence for 'God', superior life forms or civilisations more intricate than our own. It may be that our entire known universe is held within a laboratory under observation in a macro world beyond the reach of our scientific endeavours or conceiving.

We can write science fiction and posit ideas, even construct religions and their systems of belief, but all this confuses and diverts us if we begin to say or even believe they are true.

Faith

The religious exhort us to exhibit faith in the absence of facts. You must believe without seeing and trust without knowing.

But why?

Why would God play hide and seek?

Would a father and mother give birth to children and then have them brought up by foster parents instructed to tell them that their real parents loved them but were hiding from them?

Of what advantage would that be to the children?

One could surmise that the real parents were disturbed individuals.

Only a warped person would choose to deprive their children of their presence while tormenting them with the knowledge of their existence.

The cruel tyrannical God

We are taught vile facts and terrible deeds about God. The worrying aspect is that people accept them.

The story of Noah describes a despicable God willing to exterminate all that exists except for a Nazi style 'Aryan' select.

The story of Abraham being asked by God to sacrifice his son Isaac is among the most warped stories that could be read to children, yet schools and churches use it in their assemblies.

God instructs the slaughter of men, women and children in systematic genocide.

God then 'sends his own son' to be murdered viciously.

No intelligent moral human being in their right mind could believe that any of these acts had anything to do with God, nor could they choose to believe in or follow such a God.

The megalomaniacal God

Believers are encouraged to worship God using prayers, hymns and various canticles. Weekly or daily Mass and the repetitive recitation of Morning and Evening Prayer drench God in adulation.

Surely all this would be tedious, even nauseating to a God?

The only people who command continuous praise and expect a fawning subservience are disturbed tyrants. Why would God want such pointless and meaningless repetition?

Even in the most devoted and loving relationship, there could be no place for this form of worship. Can you imagine sitting in a room day after day while your partner or indeed all the people who knew you filed in and recited a script about how much they loved you?

Some argue that worship is not for God but for us. Unwittingly they have revealed the intention to control and exercise power that lies at the heart of organised religion. As though we needed to be disciplined and organised and taught by repetitive ritual. The same approach is taken by states like North Korea, where mass displays of ritualised order promote coerced obedience and send alarm through the free world.

When we look more closely at the language of prayer it makes no sense. We beseech, beg and implore God for mercy; we refer to God as King, Lord, Ruler and Sovereign; we petition and implore God to hear our prayers and we sign off with obsequious deference and in humility as obedient servants.

Do we actually believe that God would not want to be merciful because God, in our view, is a distant royal from whom we have to cajole favour and 'be ever so humble' in the process?

The lazy couch potato God

What does God do?

Like a Father Christmas figure, is God aware of every person's needs and situations and so is hard at work bringing them comfort, assistance and fulfilling their dreams?

We find that just as the Santa story begins to lose credibility as children mature, so too this job description for God.

What is Father Christmas going to leave beside the child dying of starvation this year? What comfort or assistance is God giving to the child dying of thirst, or homeless, or mutilated by bombs or afflicted with Aids or heroin addiction?

Countless people give their lives trying to eradicate or

alleviate these problems. They muster every resource available in the process, at times enduring personal suffering, sometimes sacrificing their lives in the process.

Desperately they try to gain funding, overcome bureaucracy and corruption and seek to enlist the help and good will of those who hold power and meanwhile, pitted against insuperable odds, they attempt to maintain their hope and belief.

Meanwhile God is described as all powerful and is worshipped as the one responsible for and in control of all creation. So why has not God resolved all these matters?

The mistake making God

If God is the designer and creator, and knows all things, how is it that all these problems have emerged anyway?

Did God mess things up?

Is God responsible for these fatal flaws?

Believers argue that free will governs the development of creation. Once started, the momentum for emerging life is continuous and we are in charge and are answerable.

It is easy to become lost, even convinced in such philosophical mind games.

Would it be acceptable for parents to leave their young children to do what they liked untended and unsupervised? If they came to harm, could the parents argue that the children had free will?

Would it be acceptable for a supervisor to leave an apprentice to operate machinery without training?

Do inventors not remain responsible for their inventions, architects for their designs, surgeons for their operations, parents for their children, employers for their employees?

If a mistake is made, the originator is liable and is required to overcome the issue.

God intended to create killers?

Believers argue that God intended us to have free will, knew the consequences would be dire, but accepted them as an unfortunate by-product of creation.

Would it be acceptable for parents to allow their children to play with knives and make their own choice as to whether to slice vegetables or cut someone's throat?

Would it be acceptable for an inventor to arm a robot and programme it to be able to choose whether to shoot people or not?

Is this Christian God a monster?

Believers describe a God, who designed creation, giving people free will, although knowing that it would go terribly wrong, and chooses not to intervene to correct the problems arising or prevent even the worst atrocities.

There is nothing to commend this portrayal of God.

Chapter 4

Tough Talk about the Bible

Confusion

Popular culture is awash with biblical references, starting from childhood with simplistic presentations of Noah's Ark, Joseph and his coat of many colours, Jonah and the whale and the Christmas nativity.

It can be very confusing. Are they true stories or fairy tales? Is the Bible of any use in today's world?

Uncomfortable reading

Every story, fact, claim and idea in the bible must be scrutinised to assess its merit and meaning. Very little of the bible is factually accurate. Most of the bible is propaganda, which must be handled carefully. Some of the bible is toxic and is so unsuitable that no child should be given a bible or allowed to read it without supervision.

Horrific stories

I have already cited the terrible story of Abraham being willing to kill his son, egged on by God. This tradition of infanticide culminates in God's willingness to send his own son to the earth to be killed. Would any parent want their children to have such role models?

What then of Lot offering his two daughters to be raped, but then instead having sex with them himself?

What about the story that God put a man called Er to death because he was wicked, then put Er's brother Onan to death because he wouldn't have sex with Tamar, Er's widow?

The horror continues. Tamar pretended to be a prostitute and had sex with Er's father, Judah, without revealing her identity and became pregnant. When Judah was told Tamar was pregnant through prostitution, he ordered her to be burned to death, relenting only when he was told that he was the father!

What about the story that God killed thousands of baby boys in Egypt?

What about the story that God commended Phineas for driving a spear so deep through an Israelite's body that it went through the body of the woman with whom he was sleeping as well.

What about the story of the Israelites, who killed every Midianite male, and brought the women and children back to Moses, only to be greeted by his anger and command that they should slaughter them all, except for any virgin girl they wanted to keep.

What about the story that God called for the systematic slaughter of all the men, women and children the Israelites encountered and ordering them to show no mercy and make no treaties with them, if they wanted to receive God's blessing.

More vile tales

What about God's messenger, Ehud who plunged his sword so deep into King Eglon's belly, that his fat covered over the handle and the sword came out of his back.

What about God's servant Jael who allured Sisera into her tent and gave him milk and allowed him to rest and then drove a tent peg through his head with a hammer.

What about Jephthah who thanked God for his defeat of the Ammonites by burning his daughter to death.

What about the Levite who stayed with his father-in-law for five days and then set out for home, stopping en route in Gibeah for the night. When threatening attackers surrounded the guest-house, he sent his 'wife' (concubine) out to them and allowed her to be raped and abused by them throughout the night. When he found her dead in the morning slumped by the guesthouse door, he cut up her body and distributed the pieces across Israel.

In retaliation for her death, the Israelites mounted an attack against Gibeah and the Benjamites and so many were slaughtered that the tribe of Benjamin was in danger of being eradicated. In compensation, the Israelites slaughtered the men, women and children of Jabesh Gilead, sparing just 400 virgin girls to offer as wives to the remaining Benjamites so they could repopulate the tribe. That wasn't enough. So they instructed the remaining Benjamites to kidnap young virgins from Shiloh to be their wives.

What about the story that Hannah weaned her baby Samuel and then abandoned him with the old priest Eli?

What about the story that Recab and Baanah stabbed Ish-Bosheth in the stomach and then cut off his head and took it to David, for David to order that their hands and feet be cut off and their bodies hung for all to see?

What about the story that God was so angry with Uzzah, whose oxen stumbled and tripped him onto the Ark, that he struck him down dead?

What about King David, regarded as a prophet, author of many of the psalms and foreshadowing Christ, who had an affair with Bathsheba. She became pregnant, so he had her husband killed and then took her as his wife.

What about the story that Amnon raped his sister, then despised her, and was murdered for it by his brother Absalom?

What about King Solomon who had 700 wives and 300 sex slaves.

What about the story that Ahab's blood was licked by the dogs where the prostitutes bathed?

What about the story of Elisha calling down a curse from God on some youngsters who were teasing him calling him a 'Baldie' so that bears emerged from the forest and tore 49 of the children to death.

What about the story that Jezebel was thrown from a window

so that her blood splattered the wall and the horses came and trampled her and the dogs devoured her until only her skull, feet and hands were left?

Do we want our children to have access to such villainous tales?

Terrible laws

What about God's laws?

We can beat slaves because they are our property and a man committing adultery must be put to death but he can have sex with a slave and be forgiven.

A man can capture a woman in war, bring her home and have sex with her and then, when bored with her, release her.

A man need just pay a fine if he causes a woman to miscarry by hitting her.

We should regard a woman as impure for 66 days if she bears a daughter but only 33 days if a son.

If sex takes place during a woman's monthly period, the lovers are to be exiled.

If a priest's daughter becomes a prostitute, she must be burned.

If a man suspects his wife of being unfaithful, but has no evidence, then the priest will give the woman a poison to drink which will permanently damage her if guilty and have no effect if not.

If our son or daughter converts to another faith, we must kill them with our own hands.

If we disobey these laws then God will make us eat our children as punishment.

Do we want such a book as the basis of our civilisation?

Sinister pledges

Are we comfortable with a God who says:

"I will pursue them with the sword, I will bring disaster upon them."

"The sword is for slaughter. Oh! It is made to flash like lightning. O sword, slash to the right, then to the left. I too will strike."

"I will send a plague upon her and make blood flow in her streets."

"I will spread your flesh on the mountains and fill the valleys with your remains. I will drench the land with your flowing blood."

"I will bring distress on the people and their blood will be poured out like dust and their entrails like filth."

Offensive Psalms

The psalms are at the heart of Christian worship. They are recited, intoned and sung in churches and cathedrals across the world daily.

They contain the following sentiments:

"God, you have struck all my enemies on the jaw; you have broken the teeth of the wicked."

"God, you hate all who do wrong. You destroy those who tell lies."

"God will sharpen his sword; he will bend and string his bow. He has prepared his deadly weapons; he makes ready his fla*m*ing arrows"

"God, you have destroyed the wicked; you have blotted out their name for ever and ever. Endless ruin has overtaken the enemy, you have uprooted their cities."

"God's soul hates the wicked and those who love violence. On the wicked he will rain fiery coals and burning sulphur; a scorching wind will be their lot."

"I pursued my enemies and overtook them; I did not turn back till they were destroyed. I crushed then so that they could not rise; they fell beneath my feet. You armed me with strength for battle; you made my adversaries bow at my feet. You made my enemies turn their backs in flight, and I destroyed my foes. I beat them as fine as dust borne on the wind; I poured them out like mud on the streets. He is the God who avenges me and who subdues nations under me."

"Break the teeth of the wicked in their mouths, O God; tear out, O Lord, their fangs."

And the most chilling of all:

"Happy is the one who seizes your children and dashes them against the rocks."

Are these emotions and responses we want to instil into our citizens?

The New Testament is unsuitable too

Herod slaughtered all the babies in Bethlehem.

Antipas is seduced by a woman's sexual dancing and grants her wish to have a man decapitated.

The central act is the mutilation, torture and murder of Jesus.

Shocking views

From the very start we are faced with unpalatable material.

Jesus warned us that saying "you fool" places us in danger of hell.

He taught that we should blind ourselves rather than lust and we should cut off our hand or our foot rather than do wrong with it.

He said we must let people hit us and steal from us.

He pressurised an enquirer to work with him rather than bury his dead father and didn't even want people to say goodbye to their families before following him.

He taught that if anyone didn't welcome his followers they would face a dreadful punishment.

He threatened that he would be the cause of family members betraying one another and killing one another. He said everyone would hate his followers.

He put the record straight "Do not suppose that I have come to bring peace to the earth. Not peace, but a sword."

He claimed that no one is worthy of him unless they love him more than their mother, father, son and daughter."

He was candid that any area he visited that did not accept him would face a terrible judgement.

He gloated over the fact that God had hidden important truths from many people.

He refused to see his mother and brothers when they visited because he said his followers were his family.

He said he spoke in stories so that some people would not be able to understand.

He said that those who did wrong things would be thrown into a furnace, where they would weep and gnash their teeth.

He said that those who followed him would be able to pick up snakes and even drink deadly poison and not be harmed.

He taught that when he returned to gather his followers, of two people in a bed, or a field, or wherever, one would be taken and the other left.

He told stories in support of unscrupulous and unfair actions: a man purchasing property while deceiving the seller about its true value; an employer paying the same wages to those who had worked a whole day as to those who had worked a few hours.

This is not the plastic sugar-coated Jesus the church presents?

The early Christians

It is a mistake to think that only the Old Testament has disturbing accounts.

Ananias and Sapphira sold their possessions to give to the local church but secretly kept a little back for themselves. When the church officials discovered their lie, they are threatened with God's anger and they both 'fall down dead' which disguises the shocking crime that they were killed by the Christians!

There are extensive arguments about whether the foreskin

should be cut from a child's penis.

We are told:

That God created us to do wrong things so that he could have mercy on us.

That if a woman prays without covering her head, her hair should be cut off.

Slaves must obey their masters.

Wives must submit to their husbands.

Everyone must obey the governing authorities, however corrupt they may be.

Women must not braid their hair or wear jewellery and expensive clothes. They must not teach or have authority over a man.

Then we read of angels and plagues, a dragon, beasts with multiple heads and a white horse, an abyss and a lake of burning sulphur.

This is a dangerous book. The problem is that most people are not aware of what is in it. There are too many words, the print is small and after all, there are bibles everywhere, so it must be safe.

How wrong we can be.

Innocent?

When you consider the actual contents of the Bible, it is bemusing that adults give them as gifts to children.

Further, if we are trying to work towards an eclectic and peaceful world, should we not resign to history a book, which is so compromised by stories of bloodshed, immorality and conquest?

Unfortunately, our cultural bias renders us affectionately disposed to the book and able to overlook its flaws. We accommodate in Christianity what we would find offensive in the holy book of another faith.

The perception of some faiths as warmongering and aggressive suddenly includes our own.

Corrupting models

Our children need to be protected. We must be brave in applying the knowledge and insights of the modern age to remove even seminal literary sources if they have the power to distort.

Images of a male God pursuing his enemies and requiring unquestioning subservience within a hierarchical world of kings and male rulers and clerics who must also be obeyed and in which women are ruled and owned are reactionary.

Images of religious fervour that take precedence over family relationships and loyalty and even laud the betrayal and killing of family members are repulsive.

Images of illness, death, perils and the power of nature being met with miracles are confusing and endangering.

Images of favouritism, elitism, hatred, destruction and vengeance are potent contaminants in establishing a better world.

A new Bible

If the few exquisite parts of the Bible are to be preserved and to help play their part in nourishing and inspiring future generations then they need to be extracted and published in a carefully edited volume. Perhaps a book that would contain the extracts of every faith and every philosophy, religious or secular, that was judged to have nourished our human quest towards the good.

Chapter 5

Tough Talk about the Church

Profligacy

Christian organisations have incalculable wealth. The Church of England alone has assets of around £6 billion. Stores of gold ingots, property for rent, large tracts of land, chunks of cities, stocks and shares in the world's major companies, shopping centres, industrial estates are just some of what Jesus' followers have managed to accumulate in his name.

The Archbishop of Canterbury enjoys a salary of £70,000 and lives in a palace, as do many of the bishops.

An Anglican cleric is given a rent-free house, access to private health care, a non contributory pension, grants towards furnishing and decorating, low interest loans for car and kitchen appliances, generous expenses, tax-free heating, lighting and cleaning, access to grants for private education and holidays.

It is such a contrast to Jesus and his lifestyle.

Power

When John Paul II died, over 200 world leaders attended his funeral. The Archbishop of Canter*b*ury dines with the Queen and the Prime Minister. Bishops sit in the House of Lords.

Is this the same religion that was begun by a rebel itinerant rabbi?

Politics consume the church. Intrigue, double-dealing, pacts and posturing are as commonplace in the Vatican as in Lambeth Palace as at Westminster.

Is this the same faith that was practiced clandestinely by persecuted minorities?

Constantine's rot

For nearly three hundred years, Christianity had no official place in society and no church buildings were built. The rapid growth of Christianity came about through the enthusiasm of its followers who would meet in small groups, in domestic and natural settings, sharing friendship and supporting one another practically and spiritually.

The vitality of those pocket communities arose from the radical message that each person had access to a God who loved them and wanted their commitment to help change the world for the better. The previous oppressive rule by religious officials with their traditions, rituals and laws had been swept away by Jesus. God's presence and power was available to everyone.

No boundary or restriction was immune from scrutiny. Christians had a bold spirit to identify and value the imperishable and to resist and challenge the flawed.

This all changed with the Edict of Milan and Constantine's gradual flirtation with and adoption of Christianity. The Emperor had glimpsed the potential within Christianity to harness the religious inclinations of the people and bring them under state control.

From persecution to pawns

The early Christians had suffered brutal oppression for decades. Now the sovereign autocrat appreciated that the maverick, volatile and unsavoury nature of the diverse religious practices within his empire could be constrained by imposing Christianity as the official Roman religion and taking control of its governance.

Christian gatherings and practice needed to be visible, supervised and regulated and to that end he set about building churches, having clerics appointed and bestowing the favours of high office and financial reward on those who served him well.

The grass root elements of protest and activism were replaced by compromise and collusion.

Constantine began work on the Old St Peter's Basilica giving this and the Lateran Palace to the bishop of Rome, affording him an extraordinary level of temporal power. Out of this, the monster of the Vatican has grown, a state, ruled by a papal monarch who lives in the apostolic palace.

Unquestioning loyalty

There is a disturbing similarity to the mass adulation and entrapment exhibited by the crowds fawning around Hitler, Mao, Stalin, Kim Jong-Il as to the Popes.

There is a more chilling difference. Whereas the temporal actions of rogue secular leaders can be exposed; the papal record, purportedly spiritual, remains inviolable. Whatever injustices or immoralities are brought to light, the power of the papacy continues unabated, on the premise that it is indefectible.

Murder, torture, the persecution of academics and theologians, the imprisonment of such as Galileo, financial corruption, money laundering, the silence during the holocaust, membership of the Hitler youth, child abuse, an age of consent of 14 – apparently nothing affects the devotion of those who have surrendered their critical faculties in a pack loyalty.

Church

Take a section of this crowd and place them in a building and what characteristics become apparent?

There is a need to be governed by God and by God's representative, which worldwide is predominantly a man.

There is a need to believe in supernaturalism.

There is a need to participate in ritualistic behaviour.

Unfortunately this encourages infantilism, antirealism and ritualism, which are obstacles to psychological and emotional maturity and full social integration.

Cultic and sectarian

There is a difference between naturally arising groups, such as the football club or bowls club. They represent the variety of human pursuits in contrast to the coerced and manufactured groups that have arisen through and are driven by a spiritual agenda.

In the first, belonging or not and the concomitant relationships are optional and if broken, cause limited distress to the member. In spiritual groups, a person's well-being on earth and prospects in heaven are at stake, so the consequences of leaving the group are far reaching.

Believers are taught that their favour with God depends on their performance in and acceptance by the group. Expulsion threatens the believer's core health and sanity, thus eroding any resolve they may have to leave, however urgent the need.

It is such a coercive pressure that lies behind such aberrations as the Jonestown massacre, when 909 people, 300 of whom were children, ingested cyanide in a mass suicide under the leadership of Rev Jones.

Even mainstream religious groups; under the licence they feel they have been given by God to convert others, have actively developed mind control and astute marketing techniques to halt the decline in church attendance.

The 'Alpha' course, promoted widely in the UK by evangelical churches, is a modern example.

A pointless pastime

The majority of members attend church for services alone. They devote a few hours each week to the practice of prayer and worship. I have argued that a God who needed us to adulate and beg her/him would indicate she/he was disturbed.

Worship is a contrived activity developed to instil conformity and regulate religious observance. It was important for Constantine and the leaders of the early church in league with him to be able to control the development of Christianity and the citizens involved.

Already groups were interpreting and practicing the faith differently. Constantine intervened with the arguments raging about Donatism and Arianism. If he wanted to ensure that the Christian religion would be a cohesive and constructive social instrument, it had to be regulated and its members taught.

Requiring regular attendance at 'school' on a Sunday, embedding groups of people into ritualised behaviour, building up a collective knowledge of particular hymns, chants and prayers and being able to instruct them during sermons about their behaviour and belief was instrumental in achieving control.

Holding Jesus hostage

The ultimate incentive to conform was the promise of access to Jesus. This was not limited to hearing about him alone but ingesting him in bread and wine. The church claimed that through special prayers of consecration these had become his 'Body and Blood'.

So sought after were these substances that the church had to regulate who had access to them and how they were handled. Any remaining after a service had either to be consumed by the priest or locked in a safe.

Regular reception of the Body and Blood of Christ was required and this further secured attendance rates.

Most educated modern minds have seen the ploys behind organised worship and no longer participate. Congregations are plummeting.

Stories to turn people away

Clerics present bible stories as actual events and the accounts as history. It is as though they are caught in a time warp unaware that the world has developed and knowledge evolved.

The suggestion that a book so markedly flawed as the Bible

should be relied upon for moral guidance and spiritual inspiration in our modern age is an insult to the analytical mind.

The death of church

All the indications are that the church as we know it today will disappear gradually.

Christian research has provided stark projections about future congregational figures. As the older generations die, their numbers will not be replaced. The majority of the young have had little or no exposure to church life and see it as irrelevant.

As the income stream dries up from congregations and public services, so religious buildings will be sold and the influence of the clergy will diminish.

However, the reserves held by the church, which enable it to have a disproportionate profile in public life today, will still fuel its existence temporarily.

It seems that churches are everywhere. However, most are tiny ghetto communities, made up of a handful of elderly or dependent individuals who have little in common with the majority and whose views are reactionary and at odds with the modern world.

The demise of the clericature

The need for events marking important rites of passage will remain as will the requirement of celebrants. The last twenty years have seen a proliferation of the means by which people have been trained and accredited to lead such experiences. One can be commissioned over the Internet or within extended and ancient liturgies. As far as the public are concerned, the means seem irrelevant, as long as the person can fulfil their wishes professionally and with integrity.

There is a virtual supermarket of choice for the consumer, from bespoke ceremonies to denominational liturgies, from al fresco events to church rituals, from home altars to cathedral sanctuaries, from stipendiary clergy to independent practitioners. People can create their ideal naming, thanksgiving, baptism, marriage, pledging, renewal, anniversary, confirmation, communion, worship, funeral, celebration of life, memorial experiences as they wish.

The clergy no longer hold sway over these important areas, nor does religion dictate what can and can't happen.

An old brand with outdated goods

The pulling power of the church for the consumer has waned.

People are not convinced that they have to attend worship and feel able to access God directly should they wish.

Subjecting themselves to an ill informed monologue comprising the 'sermon' each week appears a waste of time.

The psychological dishonesty of the confessional has been exposed.

The requirement to put a round wafer on your tongue seems bizarre.

Exposure to a prejudiced and discriminatory community whose practices and culture reflect a bygone age presents a threat rather than an advantage.

Chapter 6

Tough Talk about Adam and Eve

Let us first make clear that there never was an Adam and Eve, nor a Garden of Eden and the world was not made in 7 days. When that is understood, then the real meaning behind the story begins to become clear.

Traditionally, we are taught to lament the great mistake made when Adam and Eve ate the apple and were expelled from their garden paradise.

However, the story is a creation myth. It imagines our origins and charts the natural progression from childhood to maturity through the knowledge that comes from discovery.

Its intention is not to present facts, rather to impart wisdom.

It teaches that infantile fantasies have to be relinquished as we engage with the harsh realities and challenges of life. It suggests that we hold within ourselves the knowledge of paradise as well as chaos and each day we make choices that place us on a relative scale between them.

There is no magic solution that allows us to abide perpetually in paradise. Our human quest requires us to leave that which is safe and known to tame that which isn't.

This mirrors our primal journey.

Created within the warmth, security and safety of the womb only to be ejected into the unknown. Then suckled and cradled in babyhood only to be separated into independence in adulthood.

An inner momentum drives us arising from the two extremes of paradise and its opposite. The longing to remain, nurtured and protected is in tension with the compulsion to explore and so acquire knowledge and progress.

The urge is always to create a new and better paradise.

...and snakes?

The presence of a 'tempting' snake in the Garden of Eden makes it somewhat less of a paradise than fundamentalists might suggest.

So Eden reflects our human experience in the presence of beauty and order. We are arrayed by competing feelings and urges. We understand the joy of having eaten because we know the pangs of hunger. If we feel the comfort of belonging, it is because we know the insecurity of exclusion.

Experience pivots on the fulcrum of opposites. The more we voyage to the extreme of anything, the more we become aware of its shadow. In religious terms when we approach God we find that Satan is in view.

Traditionally, the apple munching was regarded as a grave mistake that doomed humanity to grub about for centuries in misery.

The story instead presents the existence of opposites as being the natural dynamic within which we conduct our lives.

Opposites

Parents have ultimate love for their children yet know the pain of having to let them go. Lovers experience the ecstasy of intimate union then face the torment of being apart. Owners of property relish their possessions but know they may be burnt or stolen. Altruists are fulfilled in their work, though by so benefiting personally they can be accused of self-interest. We experience life and root into its experience, creating a network of meaningful and life-enhancing relationships, being productive and wanting to make a positive difference that imbues it with meaning and significance. However, all this presages death and the greater our embrace of life, the deeper will be the loss at the grave.

Such opposites, *f*ar from being unhelpful, maintain our well-being and perspective. They are safety measures to maintain and protect.

Parents contain a suffocating love. Lovers come back down to earth. Possessions are not to be relied upon. Altruists are humbled. Life is seen to be precious. The greatest life will end.

Traditionally, the snake Satan slithers out from the darkness of this shadow opposite world to perform evil and is presented in a fundamentalist reading of the story as the enemy to be destroyed.

Satan, a friend of God

The author of Job, another biblical story, tries to explain that Satan has a worthy occupation and represents a vital function. Far from being the outcast, he has regular briefings with God.

Satan's work is well illustrated with Adam and Eve. They inhabit an artificial world that is stagnant – a world of perfection that leaves them dissatisfied (and so is imperfect) because though aware of the shadows, they are prevented from researching them.

In the story Satan is sent to spur them on, to harness their experience of dissatisfaction to goad them to seek greater knowledge and experience and so to fulfil their 'birthright' of being made in God's image; for God knows about good and evil and so should they.

If parents thought their children were not developing would they not seek advice? Would they not plan ways of stimulating them to grow and to explore the world around them?

Do not parents realise that their children must leave home at some point for their own good?

Satan appeals to Adam and Eve's desire to learn and to discover and he challenges the rules that they believe have been set for them.

Breaking boundaries

The shadow world of opposites that warns of loss, pain, regret, and destruction should be a constructive influence.

However, when it exerts too great a cautionary pull we over legislate and become so rule bound that risk taking and adventuring are taboo. We make ourselves too safe and become sluggish and dissatisfied.

The dynamic that rescues us, is our innate curiosity to discover what lies beyond. It comes to tempt, arouse and allure us into action. It provides us with the cheek and confidence to breach our boundaries.

But then all hell breaks out...

The story catalogues the indignities and horrors of life outside the garden, after Adam and Eve's expulsion. The best-known part is the account of their son Cain, killing his brother Abel.

It seems to present a vivid contrast between life in the womb and life after birth, life in paradise and life outside it. One cannot return, nor should we want to. The best of life today exists because babies are born and the apple is eaten continually.

In fact, there is no 'paradisiacal' stage where life hasn't been costly.

Life in the womb appears halcyon, but up to 500 million brother or sister spermatozoa perished on the journey towards the ovum. The comfort of the one is based on the slaughter of the millions.

The evolutionary process is merciless and ruthless, regarding life as expendable in pursuit of progress.

Willing victims

It is an approach we understand. History is replete with examples of explorers who have given their lives, epitomised in the death of the seven astronauts who perished when the space shuttle Columbia disintegrated on re-entry in 2003.

Unwilling victims

More chilling are the statistics for which humanity is responsible.

95 million died in the two world wars.

20 million died under Stalin's regime.

45 million died under Mao's regime.

1 million died under Kim Jong-il's regime.

It has been estimated that 231 million people were killed in the twentieth century 'by human decision'.

Reason to hope?

Not much sign of a paradise?

We have also witnessed astonishing global achievements

Talking globally, 83% now have access to clean water. 86% have enough food. 98% have a home. Child mortality is in decline. Life expectancy is rising. Deaths from Malaria and Tuberculosis are falling. Immunisation programmes have increased. Over 80% of the world's children are being educated. 75% of homes have access to electricity. Over 5 billion cell phones are in use. Over 2 billion have access to the Internet.

The slow ascent

Real engagement with life's complexities requires courage, honesty and patience. Magic and miracle are the comforting pretensions of childhood, which adults revert to under duress or to avoid responsibility. They cannot be considered serious solutions.

Have they ever proffered help to the plight of the innocent, such as the children that were gassed during the holocaust, that were born as heroin addicts or that were vaporized at Hiroshima?

When divers searched the Costa Concordia to retrieve bloated decomposed bodies there was no magic wand to wave. When war crime investigators exhume the bodies from mass graves to identify them and return them to their families there is no miracle short cut to the harrowing work.

What is clear is that every human achievement to which one can point has been the result of an extraordinary application of effort, energy and enterprise. The culmination of a process of endeavour, to which many have contributed which results in discovery, knowledge, solution, invention, stability, growth and improvement for the common good.

At times the mistakes, the destruction, the debris, even the human sacrifice which such progress has involved are found to be disproportionate and unacceptable, but predominantly it seems that you cannot create without having destroyed something.

What is clear

Life involves leaving the womb, leaving the fantasies of childhood, and leaving the safe parameters and rules of adulthood in order to participate in the common quest to establish a balanced, ordered and equitable world of justice and peace for all.

In order to achieve this we have to penetrate the mysteries of the world and the human condition to understand its potential for good and for evil.

Reading the Adam and Eve story with such an approach can release its meaning and make it a useful myth. However, because the church has presented it for centuries as factual, it has lost its opportunity to convey its wisdom in our scientific age. This needn't be a cause for regret. In its place have come countless alternative narratives in the arts that bear the same message in today's idiom with equal strength.

Films, novels, plays, poetry, songs and newspaper articles can convey the same message vividly and ingeniously.

Chapter 7

Tough Talk about Mary and the Nativity

The traditional nativity scenes performed in schools all over the country at Christmas are fantasies. While they are often wonderful, tearjerking, romantic and sentimental experiences, they are not accurate presentations of what happened.

Some may argue that it doesn't matter. It is so innocent we can all unite and delight in the beauty and the simplicity of a tale so full of mystery and magic.

They fail to realise the deceit implicit in this approach, nor the fact that it obscures the real challenges at the heart of the narrative.

No news to report

It is likely that nothing was known about the events surrounding the birth of Jesus, not least because nothing remarkable had taken place.

Joseph and Mary had created a child together called Jesus.

Jesus is around 30 when he comes to public attention and people express surprise that the carpenter's son, who they have known inconsequentially for three decades is causing such a commotion.

Fiction

Retrospectively, the religious writers create fictional accounts to convey their beliefs about Jesus. This accounts for the number of inaccuracies and contradictions within the different Gospel accounts, about even the most significant events.

The suggestion that Mary was a virgin, that a census caused Joseph to travel to Bethlehem, that three wise men brought gifts to the baby Jesus and that Herod the Great ordered the killing of the new born are all regarded as fictional references to earlier biblical writings or prevailing religious themes.

The virgin birth

Religious people fidget if you ask them what they believe about the conception of Jesus.

Did God impregnate Mary with 'his' sperm for Mary's ovum.

Did God impregnate Mary with a zygote?

How did whatever happened occur? By magic? With the help of an 'angel'? Normally?

How was Jesus conceived?

If a stronger person coerced Mary, didn't this constitute a rape?

If we unpack the narrative and try to extract the religious spin, we might reveal a variety of well-known predicaments.

A young unmarried woman, Mary, became pregnant. When her partner Joseph discovered, his first reaction was to split up with her, but knowing that in those times especially, her future would have been exceptionally bleak, he stayed with her. If we want to deepen the dilemma, perhaps while engaged to Joseph, she had an affair and become pregnant, and despite this they stayed together and he brought up the child as his own.

However, it is even more likely that Joseph and Mary conceived Jesus naturally and according to social custom.

Speculation

Theologians have sought fruitlessly to explain the belief in a supernatural origin.

Words can be used to sound out complex ideas like 'a virgin birth', Jesus being 'fully human and fully divine', the baby being 'God on earth' and the physical manifestation of 'the second person of the trinity', but they are sounds without any factual or objective rationale. They purport to convey a meaning but it is one rooted in fantasy rather than knowledge.

Is Christmas a charade?

Setting aside the schmaltz and the fantasy, watching a school nativity can be uncomfortable viewing. The children are being indoctrinated into a cultural and religious worldview that is partisan and divisive.

The story is presented that it was to us, to our faith, family, culture, school, land that God was born, and continues to be born and the entire world will come and be like us and worship him.

This trite and unhelpful take on the biblical narrative, which endures from the school stage to the adult heart, is typically selective.

It conceals the inhumane and abusive parts of the story. Mary's rape, Mary's suffering on the journey and in the stable, the slaughter of the surrounding children and Mary and Joseph's terrified escape into Egypt don't feature.

So, if we suck the sugar and bin the lemon and if all of it is bogus anyway and if it perpetuates a biased and offensive view of God then why do we do it?

Let's move on

When Constantine adopted Christianity he chose not to erase the prevailing religious, culture rather adapt and progress it.

The celebration of Jesus conquering death was attached to the pagan spring festivals with Easter emerging as a name after the pagan deities such as Eostre. The celebration of the birth of Jesus was fixed to coincide with Saturnalia, the most important festival of the Roman year to the God Saturn.

In fact many of our religious customs, which we assume, are ours and Christian are not.

People gave gifts and decorated their homes at 'Christmas' time and eggs and rabbits were associated with spring before Jesus was born!

People made the sign of the T over their chests in honour of Tammuz, the Sumerian God. They ate 'hot T buns' marked with the letter.

Gods and Goddesses died having been hung from nails and descended to the underworld only to be resurrected.

Forty days of mourning preceded the festivals marking their deaths.

It is probable that every religious practice, rite and tradition has links across the world and history with other faiths. Humanity is entangled within a web of finite methods and beliefs of ha*n*dling religion. There is nothing unique.

Ancient practices

The intriguing question perhaps is whether modern enlightened society can find a way of re-presenting and practicing these ancient festivals and faiths.

At the heart of the Christmas experience is the celebration of birth, upon which our life depends. It sees the gathering of our loved ones with whom we share our lives and the mutual expression of appreciation in the giving of gifts.

This does not require a Jesus.

In fact the concentration of attention on Jesus is problematic, changing what should be an inclusive festival into one that requires allegiance to or tolerance of a particular religious and cultural tradition.

It also perpetuates prejudice.

That one baby is more special than another because of their origins;

That special babies should receive preferential treatment;

That everyone should bow down and worship this baby;

That the special baby happens to be male;

That the Christian view prevails over all others.

Special babies

Jesus is not the only remarkable person ever to have been born. Every age produces extraordinary individuals who make their mark, alter the course of history and contribute substantially to the common good. We laud their lives.

At birth, a child's destiny remains a mystery. There was no virgin birth, angel choirs or visiting kings at the birth of Socrates, Cleopatra, Newton, Darwin, Pocahontas, Catherine the Great, William Wilberforce, Vivekananda, Mahatma Gandhi, Rosa Parks, Benazir Bhutto, Nelson Mandela and Aung San Suu Kyi.

We express our desire to honour their work and memory in various ways, but not by deifying them or constructing revisionist myths about their early lives.

The modern mind finds such an adulteration of the truth offensive. We want to know and understand the facts rather than be deceived by fiction.

The myth makers

However, the ancient practice of gloss and spin persists in the airbrushing of photographs and our obsession with celebrities. We are manipulated by the advertising industry and fall prey to the ploys of branding, cosmetic surgery and the world of artificiality.

There are many who still promulgate myths that reduce rather enhance our lives. Much of what we read in the press is distorted, exaggerated or false.

Clever columnists and glossy magazine writers are expert in stretching an ordinary set of circumstances into dazzling headlines and punchy paragraphs. At the first read, it can seem that those written about or photographed live a different existence to our own in which their circumstances and experiences take on magical proportions.

On closer reading, stripping away the hyperbole and focussing on the raw facts, the stories are often risible in their inconsequential nature. Far from being magical, we realise we are being tricked today by these modern tales as we have been by the ancient biblical stories.

Christmas, stripped bare

Instead why don't we marvel each year at the 'miracle' of birth and the innocence of childhood?

Let us pause from our endeavours and the pressures and preoccupations of adulthood.

We can still relish our children's school nativity play.

However, in the crib, let each school rotate the identity of the babe.

One year, just an anonymous babe, who will live an unremarkable and ordinary life upon the earth.

Another year, one of the countless babes who grew up and made their mark upon history. Beethoven, Saladin, Anne Frank, Chien-Siung Wu, Martin Luther King, Vijaya Lakshmi Pandit…

Another year, a baby born in our lifetime, still alive today who is living a notable life helping others and making a beneficial difference to our world.

Gifts and love

Gifts express the gratitude and appreciation we feel towards our nearest and dearest as well as towards those with whom we work and upon whom we rely. The generosity of giving promotes a sense of well-being and encourages us to include those more remote from us and to consider the plight of the poor and suffering.

Opening our pockets, purses and bank accounts as well as our hearts for other people is an important annual ritual that saves us from a selfish introspection and re-engages us with those around us.

Decorations

Embellishing homes, trees and public spaces marks a time of celebration and holiday. It unites communities and nations in a common act of creativity. It interrupts the mundane with occasion and provides the stimulus to prepare and participate in a different way of engaging with life.

All work and no play makes us very dull and life tedious.

Fluctuation and variety, just as tilling the ground, aerates our lives and maintains the cycle of fertility.

Binge and banquet

Responsibility and balance in all things are at the heart of public education. Personal discipline, moderation, and a healthy lifestyle are the apsirations politicians and ministers uphold.

The majority of us are dutiful and contribute to a well-ordered society.

One of the rewards to which we look forward, which were much rarer for previous more pressed generations, are those times we can climb off our everyday conveyor belts and relax in the slipstream of a holiday or a special season.

Christmas, Mother's Day, Easter, Father's Day, bank holiday weekends, the summer holidays, Halloween, Bonfire night... we take every opportunity to reap the benefits of our hard work; and enjoying special drinks and foods with family and friends lies at the heart of our relaxation.

Changing the name

Learning to adopt inclusive language has been an uncomfortable challenge for many people. Human beings are obstinate by nature and cling fearfully to the familiar.

It is anachronistic to describe the national December festivities as Christmas.

The majority of participants do not attend 'mas(s)' and do not understand their celebrations in honour of 'Christ'.

So many atheists, agnostics and adherents of all the faith traditions share the holiday season, give gifts and decorate their homes, but it has nothing to do with Jesus for them. They continue the traditions which have operated for centuries and are unrelated to Christianity.

Perhaps we should call it Noeltide, the time to express the joy of birth.

Chapter 8

Tough Talk about Easter and the Resurrection

We must be specific. Jesus died. His flesh began to putrefy. His body was buried. Did this same man, with the same body and the same flesh come back to life? The answer is a simple and clear No.

Even the Bible doesn't make this claim

Instead stories arose about various people's experiences in relation to Jesus after his death. Every bereavement counsellor will have heard similar stories.

People speak of having heard, seen and even touched their loved ones after death. Not everyone has such encounters. It appears that certain people translate their grief into such intimate manifestations of the bereaved.

The biblical and present day anecdotes all represent the loved one as being in many ways similar to how they were prior to death but in other ways different.

The most notable difference is they are not able to present their loved one in public, or have them independently or scientifically assessed or have their existence verified in any objective evidential manner.

The physicality of their loved one after death is inaccessible.

The contradictions

The inconsistencies between the various accounts of the crucifixion and resurrection leave us many puzzles.

Was Jesus crucified on the Wednesday, Thursday or Friday? Were his legs broken? Did someone help him carry his cross or even swap places, being crucified instead of Jesus?

Were there earthquakes and did the rocks shatter? Was the temple veil, some 20 metres high and 10 cms thick, ripped from top to bottom? Did graves burst open and the dead spring back to life?

Why are there so few non-Christian references to his death?

The empty tomb

Did Pilate decide it prudent to steal the body of Jesus to prevent his tomb becoming a shrine? Did some of the disciples remove the body to support the belief in his resurrection?

Regarding him as God's sacrificial lamb, did the disciples cremate him on one of the numerous fires around Jerusalem, lit to burn the remnants of the lamb eaten during the Passover celebrations?

If another was crucified in his place, did Jesus or his helpers remove the body?

What we do know is that the body in the tomb went missing and either in the grief delerium that followed many stories were spawned about the bereaved's experiences of encountering him or if Jesus was still alive, having been taken down from the cross, or if another had taken his place, then a variety of appearances could have been orchestrated.

Meaningless

Whatever the range of possible scenarios, one thing is clear. There is no objective evidence that Jesus rose bodily from the dead. In fact the Christian church has led their believers haplessly down a nonsensical cul-de-sac.

So ludicrous is the belief in the bodily resurrection of Jesus, that having stated he rose from the tomb, the early disciples have to dispose of his resurrected body which they do in the contrived story of the ascension. Forty days after Easter Sunday we are told Jesus ascends into heaven in a cloud.

If we are honest, these stories, even if we wanted to believe them, do not help us with a belief in resurrection.

Our loved ones die. Their bodies putrefy. They are cremated and become ash or are interred and if exhumed years later are a collection of bones. If we want to believe that they are in fact reclothed in a new body in heaven, then the stories about the missing body of Jesus, his empty tomb, 40 days of earthly appearances and then a cloud transit to heaven don't help.

Resurrection stories

Unsurprisingly, stories of the dead rising to new life abound in ancient cultures. They still do in our own. Many modern films play with the theme and explore the reaches beyond death.

The public's insatiable appetite to penetrate the mystery of death maintains a burgeoning psychic market and leaves the majority susceptible to the arts of mediums and priests. Pseudo-scientific documentaries have become increasingly popular that investigate the supernatural and claim to film the appearances of ghosts or spiritual occurrences.

None have been verified independently.

The Derren Brown phenomenon

We are beginning to appreciate the limitations of the human mind and how easy it is to manipulate and predict human behaviour.

Our brains are programmed to handle data in particular ways. At times this means we are incapable of accurate observation because the programme our brain is following overrides the reality.

A good example of this involves railway tracks. The brain is programmed to reduce the size of objects according to their distance from us. Looking to the horizon or looking down a set of railway tracks confirms this.

Artists use a technique called 'one-point perspective' to replicate this, so that an object like a road or train tracks recedes in the distance to one spot.

However, if an artist draws a set of tracks, but maintains their width from the foreground of the picture to the background, when you view their work, the brain will override the artist's painting and see the tracks as narrower in the background.

Even if you measure the tracks and thereby inform your brain that they are the same width, the brain will not allow the eyes to see this.

My eyes played tricks on me

Science tells us that the eyes send partial data to the brain, partly in response to expectation and the brain processes this in relation to stored data and creates a unified image.

A simple demonstration of this is how hard it is to see someone if they are not wearing what you expected.

A more frightening example is when you see something that is not there. This may happen in the twighlight but can as easily occur in the middle of the day. You are not focussing on a particular area, although it is within your field of vision.

A thought comes to you or a movement occurs related to that peripheral zone, and your brain superimposes a possible image into it. Perhaps it is a cat leaping or an attacker lurking. The moment you focus, the image disappears or is clarified to be not a cat leaping but a branch swaying, not an attacker lurking but a pile of cardboard.

The brain is in control of what we see. So much so, that if we wore glasses that inverted our vision, the brain, detecting a fault in the programme, would re-invert the image.

My ears play tricks as well

Once you become sensitive to the brain filling in the gaps and making sense of sensory experiences you can observe the process.

While concentrating on something else you hear a series of indefinable sounds. The brain then suggests a sentence, almost like predictive texting.

Someone unaware of this mental facility may well be alarmed or awed believing that someone, even God has spoken to them. Once alerted, you can catch the words and actually retrieve the sounds that lay behind them and dismiss the brain's suggestion in the same way you can reject the smartphone's suggested word.

Many people will talk about how they saw something or heard someone and are sure it was real. For them it was. Their brain gave them the experience, perhaps the face or body or voice of their deceased loved one. However, it didn't actually happen. No one else could have observed it. The data arose from the brain.

Recently I was asked to help a couple. The woman was adamant that her husband berated her regularly when she woke up during the night. It had happenend again the night before I saw them. The husband, knowing this not to be true, unbeknown to his wife had set up a recording device. The wife was astonished when no sounds had been recorded throughout the night.

The capacity for our brains to produce experiences for us that are vividly real is something we are just beginning to realise.

Dozing dreams

It is disconcerting when you find yourself in that hinterland behind the edge of waking still immersed in a dream.

The contours of consciouness become confusing and blurred and the dream's characters and emotions spill out, accompanying you as you wake.

We do not know we are alive when we fall asleep. We 'die' every night to be reborn in the morning. Nevertheless, our nocturnal adventures can be legendary, most of which remain inaccessible to us though a few potent images linger.

The brain indeed has a 'mind of its own' to which we are subject.

What we observe as real may be an illusion, a figment of our imagination, an image that the brain has produced, a model our species has arrived at for managing our surroundings.

Beyond us

The truth is we only see and hear a small part of what exists and what we see and how we hear is packaged to suit our species.

When we enter the macroscopic world of multiverses, light years and black holes or the sub-atomic world of bosons, tau neutrinos and quarks we realise our finitude.

We see what we need to see for our own protection and survival, mainly complex collections of particles, molecules and chemical bonds that the light scattered around has made detectable. We see the big picture in relation to the tiny world and the small picture in relation to the vast world, but it all amounts to a tiny slice of reality.

As science continues to reveal the enormity of what we do not know and gives ever clearer accounts of what we do, then the religious language that we use comes under a ruthless scrutiny. Religious people can no longer rely upon unsubstantiated platitudes as the basis of a belief.

Dispelling the myths

There is no incontestable evidence that Jesus was crucified. There is no reliable evidence that his body came back to life or that people had physical encounters with him.

What we do know is that a group of people established a movement based on their post-bereavement experiences that led them to believe that Jesus was still alive. In the hysterical, unscientific, religion-driven world of their day, the ground was fertile for this new faith to grow exponentially.

Many modern educated believers understand the resurrection differently. The cycle of life that follows a death; the re-awakened body of believers that spread the Gospel; the ability to translate evil and destruction into good and creativity; the tenacity of life as a more potent force than death.

Divisive belief

The unfortunate consequence of requiring adherence to specific dogmas such as bodily resurrection is that it alienates.

A message of universal love, hope, forgiveness and redemption becomes the posession of the few, packaged according to their sights as 'Christianty', rather than a gift to all.

Then, that few develop complicated rituals and modes of observance to commemorate the events which gave rise to 'their' faith; none more so than the Holy Week and Easter liturgies. They can be mystical and awe inspiring but are so rareified that they remain inaccessible unless one is steeped in Christian culture or the observance is so dumbed down as to become facile.

The concentration on Jesus is offensive

Every year, decade, century worshippers re-enact the passion of Christ, whether dramatically or liturgically. Prayers, tears and continuous services mark the last days and hours of Christ's life.

Why?

What was so special about the suffering and death of Jesus?

It may be helpful to regard his fate as a paradigm highlighting the innocent suffering of a prisoner of conscience, but to focus each year on the same story is gratuitous.

What about the millions of people who, since Christ, have suffered equally and indeed far more, whose stories aren't told and whose memory has been allowed to be forgotten?

What about the thousands of people who are suffering today, even at this moment, for whom no one is campaigning and for whom no special service is being held?

It is an insult to their plight that Christians focus so single mindedly on Jesus alone.

Particularly when Jesus suffered unnecessarily out of his religious fervour. He was not campaigning for the rights of others, nor resisting an evil aggressor. He did not die for a noble cause or defending another. He was complicit in his death, understanding that it would lead him to paradise.

Is it not foolhardy to continue to uphold such an example of misguided religious fervour when we are trying to bridle the irrationality of people's religious motivation for exacting violence on others and on themselves?

Shouldn't our concentration and our honouring be of those who have suffered and are suffering on behalf of others, in their campaign for the human rights of others and in defence of others?

Updating the Christ figure

There have been and are so many saviour figures. It would be far better if every year churches chose a different person's life to highlight. Most pressing would be the lives of present day prisoners of conscience or the oppressed.

The Holy Week services could focus prayers around their situation.

The Easter services could reflect the passion and commitment of the community to spread information about the person's situation and campaign to help secure their well-being and the well-being of all who are suffering.

This would make riveting and relevant worship.

I suspect that many worshippers might object, because their adulation of the suffering Christ has very little to do with Jesus or his predicament all those years ago or his life today. Instead it is a self-centred psychodrama in which they satisfy their need for personal reassurance and affirmation.

In fact, his suffering has been so sanitised and has become so remote, that congregations watching Mel Gibson's explicitly violent film, 'The Passion of Christ' remained unaffected. God had sanctioned it all, Christ was fulfilling his role, they were the beneficiaries and there were no need for tears.

In truth we need to be drowning in the tears pouring from us at the suffering of the world and straining every fibre of our being to devote our lives in resurrecting all that is dead and dying around us.

Chapter 9

Tough Talk about Heaven

The most traumatic events of our lives involve the death of our loved ones.

We are engulfed in disbelief when a relationship that has formed the bedrock of our lives is over. Life as we knew it has been shattered irretrievably. The unalterable finality is chilling.

Within this overwhelming realisation the need to locate an escape mechanism is urgent and the language of heaven comes readily to mind.

Even entrenched atheists can incline towards thoughts of another existence when faced with the brutality of death.

So what of heaven?

The inescapable problem, however, is that while reference to heaven can offer a superficial palliative, its effectiveness under scrutiny is a mere placebo. The ideas, beliefs and speculations that form part of the heaven package are ill formed and unsatisfying.

Religionists describe an unending existence where we are caught in a repetitive cycle of worship and adulation of a deity. An objective assessment of such an image would highlight concern at the entrapment by a greater power of those kept in perpetual servitude. It seems more a vision of hell.

In popular culture, heaven is depicted as a selective continuation of life in which the best parts are preserved and the inferior aspects shed. Often the scenarios that are envisioned involve reunions with loved ones followed by variations on people's dreams and fantasies of an idyllic existence.

What is apparent immediately is that the scope of our imagination appears limited to our earthbound existence and that our projections about paradise are cursorily drawn. In fact, they lack any realistic evaluation.

After the reunions, what happens next? After waking up in silk sheets under an azure sky what next? After lying on a beach sipping cocktails what follows?

If we extend our view just a little we begin to face reality.

Will we have to grow our food, shop, cook, eat, drink, wash-up and exercise?

Will we have to attend educational classes?

Will we be able to play sport or watch sport?

Will we be able to be entertained or entertain?

Will we have friends?

Will we fall in love, be reunited with our earthly love… or loves?

Will we make love?

Will we have children?

Or is heaven a totally different existence?

If so, are we still ourselves or are we an amalgamation of others?

Do we have bodies or are we spirits alone?

The minute we venture down the different route we stumble into three problems.

First, that it is very hard to imagine any form of realistic existence that could be fulfilling other than improvements of our earthly lives.

Second, that the more different it becomes the less of a comfort it can be to the bereaved.

Third, that once we begin to slide into speculation we are in the realm of science fiction. Some enthusiasts appear able to cleave to such fictional accounts of the future and even to build their lives around them, but they offer little assistance when trying to come to a considered view of the afterlife.

Perfection

The most alluring image is of a world perfected, where war, conflict and personal enmities are all absent, where justice and peace are known throughout and all are fulfilled.

There is a fatal flaw to such an image.

If there is such an existence in another dimension then there is no moral justification for having exposed humanity to the suffering known on earth. It is insufficient to argue that earth is a preparatory experience for what lies beyond, because the course of our lives is random and clearly there is no uniformity to what each person learns.

Chapter 10

Tough Talk about Prayer

You don't need to read a paper if you attend church. The daily intercessions are a list of the world's woes, mawkishly repeated in sombre tone. The purpose of the exercise is never discussed.

Some have justified prayer as being the directing of the faithful to the relevant issues of the day. Surely, if they were 'faithful' they would be well versed in the suffering and plight of others. If *not*, then being nudged in church is unlikely to galvanise their attention, much more to salve their consciences by suggesting they can leave the problem at God's door.

Why do we pray?

There is an illogicality about prayer. If God is benevolent and merciful then we would not need to pray. God would have anticipated our needs and the world's needs and provided wisely.

The argument that it is instructive and beneficial for us to identify need and intercede is unconvincing. Needs are legion and identifying the best ways to manage them is a basic human requirement. Prayer that looks to God for a solution would only make sense if it could be shown to be effective.

Does prayer work?

If you mean, does God intervene and alter the course of events in response to our prayers, then it must be a resounding 'No'.

Don't be shaken or even surprised by this. It would be horrifying if the answer had been yes. What sort of a monster would God be if he/she could rescue us but refrained and watched our suffering.

When we are aware of a person's plight, a good person will yearn to do all they can to help, devoting whatever resources they have available to do so. Many risk their lives and sacrifice their comforts to immerse themselves in trying to make the world a better place.

The thought that all this noble human endeavour is taking place while God just watches from the sidelines, withholding his/her ability to resolve the problems is repugnant.

It is also offensive to believe that you can pull strings in high places because you are a believer and on God's side or that by repeated pestering prayer you can twist God's arm up his/her back and irritate or impress God so much that he/she helps.

The divine lottery

Believers claim that God is able and wants to help but needs us to pray first or pray within the correct belief system or pray in the proper manner. The onus is placed on us to discover the correct method of gaining access to this divine rescue service. As though we needed to phone, but didn't know the correct number.

Meanwhile, children die of dysentry on pavements in the developing world and have their legs blown off by land mines and are tortured and maimed and God does nothing, because we are still fumbling for the number and haven't made the prayer call. However, even if we had, the outcomes wouldn't have altered.

The fundamentalist believer opines that if only the child had been a particular kind of believer and prayed in the correct way, then God would have saved them. In truth, God does not intervene.

Suffering

The state of the world and the acute suffering of so many not only militates against the notion of God being able to act but also raises a philosophically insuperable hurdle to belief.

The believer's argument that everyone is given free will is a vacant riposte. The destitute, murdered, raped, cancer ridden, blind and tortured are unable to exercise their free will. The aborted child or one born with HIV or drug dependency was given no choice and enjoyed no divine protection. Nature's ruthless evolutionary momentum shows no moral pattern or purpose and no divine governance.

The arbitrary and colossal waste involved in reproduction and development is chilling.

Against this background of horror and expendability we create a miniscule comfort zone within which we tuck ourselves physically and appease ourselves morally and fantasise spiritually.

God creates and cares. We are good and altruistic. Creation is benign and manageable.

The evident facts are that there is no God and if any more complex being is found to exist, he/she exhibits no care. Few are good and altruism is rare and creation is perilous and uncontrollable. Disordered energy becomes ordered only to become again disordered. We appear and disappear. We live and die.

Is prayer a waste of time?

Yes. The root meaning of the word 'prayer' is to obtain by begging. We have argued that no amount of begging will effect one jot or tittle of change.

Prayer though takes many forms.

Repetitive, disciplined prayer as practiced in religious houses or in the daily recitation of the Divine Office or in the prayer cycles of the various faiths may promote self-discipline but it also absorbs resources and panders to an obsessional need for routine.

Where it forms a resource for a community otherwise engaged in social outreach it can play a vital resourcing role, though other models would be equally, even more effective. Where it is an end in itself, providing purpose and shelter for a closed community, it is only effective in placating, concealing or frustrating the needs of the participating individuals.

Meditative prayer and silence can provide the necessary space for creative thinking, self-discovery and strategic planning but these benefits are self-resourcing and can be obtained without the element of prayer.

Where there are benefits arising from prayer, they are the consequences of a human activity in which God plays no active part.

In fact, the disadvantages begin to accumulate when you introduce God. The supplicant, despite conclusive evidence, persists in the belief that a supernatural force will enhance the prospects of their prayer being answered. They feel less responsible for the outcome and less committed to facing the reality of the issue.

Into that amorphous situation creeps dishonesty. Believers enter a world of euphemism which obscures the challenges and requirements that must be faced. They say that God will bring healing, the poor will be helped, the flood victims rescued, the oppressed will be comforted, but they don't say how or when and they never monitor whether their claims are borne out.

If the sick die, the poor starve, the victims drown and the oppressed's plight continues then there is no enquiry or compensation claim lodged at heaven's door.

Scientific salvation

M-theory is a collection of the different ways by which we observe existence. There is no single 'theory of everything' but what is apparent is that everything is connected, often paradoxically.

Miracles abound in the Bible and believers are urged by their preachers to expect them and pray for them. But there is no intellectual caveat provided by M-theory to suggest that miraculous interventions have a place.

No miracle has been independently scientifically verified. It is not possible to alter the underlying complex laws that govern the connections of the physical world to effect a desired change. Understanding enables us to learn to manipulate them to our advantage but only through empirical procedures.

We have walked on the moon, split the atom and developed IVF but all our achievements have involved analytical research. They are the true wonders that deserve our awe and worship.

If people re-allocated the time they spend in prayer to learning and research then the phantom miracles promised by their pastors for the 'believing elect' would become real wonders in the world today available for everyone.

We are alone

Often our greatest fear is being alone. However, we are always.

We inhabit a skin and walk separate from all others. The experience of such estrangement contrasts with the intimacy of our gestation in our mother's womb. We seem never to overcome the sense of our displacement at birth.

During infancy we instinctively remain close to our mother and father, at school to our friends, in adolescence our group or gang, in courtship to our partners. It is a perpetual flight from solitude.

We must be in communication with others to affirm our sense of existence, identity and well-being. Modern devices enable us to be in touch 24/7. Survey a train or pavement, a shopping mall or park. Everyone is texting, phoning, emailing or chatting. It's a world of words that form bridges across which we can feel connected and so safe.

God – the eternal conversation

The battery fails, the person says goodbye, sleep beckons and that devastating darkness of oblivion engulfs us.

Some reach for the radio, music, even go to sleep with the TV playing; anything to remove the silence and give the impression of company.

Some people begin talking to themselves audibly, at times not even being aware that they are.

However, everyone talks to themselves inaudibly.

As though the idea we could be alone is so untenable to human consciousness that we create the facility to communicate.

The language becomes intriguing. Do we say 'I am thinking' or 'I am having a conversation with my thoughts'? Are we and our thoughts one and the same, although the process of thinking is like a conversation?

What then do we mean by our conscience?

Is our conscience part of our thoughts or does it form a separate voice within the chatter of our minds?

So far it seems as though there may be one, two or three strands to this conversation. We may want to add our feelings as a fourth.

However, if all of this is too centred in ourselves and so fails to alleviate our loneliness, it is a small step to choose to 'identify' one of the voices within us as the voice of another, 'God', which we see as coming from outside ourselves, to which we give an appropriate divine or spiritual name.

The moment of conversion

When someone discovers this 'outside voice' facility it is an immense psychological experience, described by many as being 'born again'.

It is as though they are re-united with their primal experince of being in continual, unbroken contact with another. Loneliness is removed and a sense of comprehensive well-being suffuses them.

The God voice 'component'.

We are parented for years; more so than any other species. Being protected, advised and guided provides us with security. We crave independence but achieve it with the loss of our primary carers.

While we assume we are self-sufficient and *in* early adulthood can display a reckless and arrogant nature, we harbour the desire to find a wise and resourceful replacement for our parents.

The 'God voice' is an attractive solution.

The divine script is largely already written, drawn from parental and other influential sources, mixed with one's own knowledge and experience. It is a conversation with one's past and future and with careful scrutiny can be appraised.

However, it is also unpredictable and unaccountable.

It can be contaminated by subliminal and subsconcious desires. Clever manipulators like Derren Brown can usurp it for entertainment. More sinister are the viral agents that can seize it for malign purposes like its radicalisation by other religionists or extremists.

Growing up

The path to maturity involves relinquishing the longing for fusion and direction and coming to terms with our solitary state.

We are responsible for what we make of our lives and circumstances and how we react to the choices and plight of others.

We belong by immersing ourselves into reality and by participating constructively in the network of relationships around us.

Our aspirations, the consequences of our actions and the morality of our motivation are all judged within the world community. There is no place for an intervening and governing deity to whom we can petition for advantage.

Chapter 11

Tough Talk about Ritual and the Mass

The point of entry into the Christian faith is symbolised by Baptism/Christening, which is adminstered to children by the main denominations. As youngsters or adults people then affirm their faith through Confirmation.

The central act of worship for Christians is the reception of bread and wine at a service called variously – the Mass, Eucharist, Holy Communion, Lord's Supper or Agape.

The purpose of ritual

The prevalence of ritualised behaviour in humans and animals is remarkable. It illustrates the use of repetitive behaviour to control and convey. From individuals to corporate life we take part in elaborate forms of stylised behaviour.

Often these are linked specifically with an immediate event making the ritual vital and relevant, such as a handshake or two-minute silence or the countdown to midnight on New Year's Eve.

At other times the link is remote and curious as in most religious ritual.

Baptism and Confirmation

Baptism and Confirmation do not effect a physical change. The flesh of those involved is unaltered; in the same way that a service of marriage has no cellular impact.

Such services express, represent and indicate something beyond themselves that may or may not exist.

A person may or may not believe, may or may not wish to be a Christian, may or may not wish to be married, may or may not love God or their partner. It is not possible to know objectively whether those involved are sincere or not.

On a countdown to New Year, in a handshake or even a two-minute silence, sincerity is not a required ingredient. The act accomplishes the task.

However, without sincerity, Baptism, Confirmation and Marriage, while achieving an objective purpose, are meaningless.

Extracting the need for sincerity

In the early days of a religious movement, sincerity is a premium ingredient. The zest and burgeoning growth relies upon the true allegiance and genuine experience at the core of those involved.

Once established, the infrastructure gives stability and endurability to the movement, so what lies in the hearts of the membership becomes less of an issue.

After decades, even centuries, the main denominations are able to maintain sufficient momentum on structure and finance alone and on*l*y a modicum or even an absence of sincerity in those involved.

Dead rituals are safer

The loss of sincerity is regarded as an advantage to the denominational moguls.

A sincere person is unpredictable, alive to their conscience, questioning and searching.

Religious leaders prefer a human being to be tamed and taught to practice the habitual rituals promoted by the church. The are baptised, confirmed and regularly receive Communion without thinking, instinctively, while at the same time giving money to the church, swelling the congregation and preserving the church's power base in society.

A subtle switch has taken place, in which the believer's loyalty is directed towards the institution and its practices and not to its origins. God and Jesus fade into the background as active components and are replaced by the cultural ethos of the community. A protest that the culture has become unchristian goes unheard, because what matters to the members is the prevailing life of the community and not its ancient origins.

Ask a regular what it's all about

Though numbers are depleting rapidly, thousands still attend Mass, still receive their bit of wafer bread and sip of wine. Why?

If you ask at the door, you'll receive a random and incoherent array of answers laden with doctrinal goobledegook.

Jesus wants us to… it's his body and blood… it's a memory meal… his last supper…

Many of the concepts are nonsensical. If you press the believer for more they dry up, grow confused, surrender or play the 'it's my faith' card – in other words – I ain't got a clue!

Why would Jesus want us to eat a bit of wafer bread each week? He never did.

How can any sane person believe it's reasonable to eat someone's flesh or drink their blood, even metaphorically?

What are they remembering and why?

What ingredients are included?

The ritual of receiving bread and wine forms the backbone of religious discipline in the traditional church.

The chosen ingredients are:

This is a meal for the few, the specially chosen, the elite, the clique, the remnant, those gathered around Jesus, the ones he loves truly.

To them he gives his life, his service, his commitment, his all.

He washes their feet and forgives their sins.

He is taking them with him to heaven.

The omitted ingredients are:

One of those attending had planned already to lead his assassins to him;

One of those attending would deny having anything to do with him;

Many of those attending did nothing to try and help him or save him.

This was the annual Jewish ritual Passover meal and had nothing to do with Christianity.

Barbaric bloodshed

The Jewish Passover marked the horrific tale of God slaughtering all the first-born Egyptian children to protect his 'chosen' people the Jews.

Onto this event is added the heinous concept that God would allow his own 'son' to be crucified and that his followers should drink his blood and eat his flesh.

It's a blood and butchery fest designed to promote exclusive community and divisive religious allegiance.

Could there be a better approach?

In contrast to this self-interested understanding of the last food Jesus shared with others is the observation that Jesus promoted something quite different.

He encouraged strangers to gather together to discuss and share ideas and when they did so in large numbers arranged for food to be distributed among them equally.

This inclusive model of community provided an instructive and distinctive alternative to the partisan norm. It was though of little use to those whose vested interests required defined boundaries and a membership encouraged by advantage.

Ritual in conflict with reality

The ritual of the Mass evolved, not because Jesus intended or wanted it, but as the product of building a new religious organisation based on his life.

The organisation took control of the Jesus brand and regulated people's access to it and use of it.

It was essential to maintain the potency of their core product and the propaganda of resurrection provided the means. The Jesus at the centre of Christianity was alive. People could still have a relationship with him. Maximising the potential, they could actually touch him and even absorb him into their bodies, thus experiencing intimate union with him.

The clerics would guard the flesh and blood of Jesus. They would lock him away in safes and make him available through a prescribed ritual which required the worshipper to attend and submit to the instruction and discipline of the church.

The ritual was shrouded in mystery, involving a strange language and specified actions and could only be performed by male priests, often out of sight and behind closed doors, authorised by male bishops and a male Pope in service to a male deity.

A far cry from anyone and everyone sharing sandwiches on a hillside with Jesus.

Mean worshippers who won't share their sweets

If people wanted to continue the legacy of Jesus' love, what could they do instead of the charade of Sunday Communion?

Surprisingly, it would not involve a church or a service or a ritual or a priest.

It would be different from those many worshippers who pour from Sunday services with the taste of wine on their lips and smugness in their hearts believing they have fulfilled all their duty towards God by receiving 'Communion' and who have no intention of doing more.

On their way home they may well pass a beggar on the pavement, a rough sleeper under a bridge, an alcoholic in a doorway, a migrant worker in the fields, a refugee selling the Big Issue, a Sikh worshipper from the Gurdwara or a prostitute being pimped by sex traffickers. They pass them all by without even a thought that the Mass had anything to do with them.

In contrast Jesus would want people to be generous and openhearted, patterning a way of life, in which they offered hospitality and welcome to family, friend and stranger alike.

They would open their home and invite to their table all and sundry without bias.

They would regard all people equally as those with whom they would eat and those for whom they would provide food and from whom they would receive food.

They would do this, knowing that those with whom they ate would represent the totality of humanity including those who would bring them blessing and those who would bring them harm, but such knowledge would not prevent their desire to model and encourage inclusive community not based on self-interest.

They would have eyes to see injustice and an inclination to redress it.

The food of love

Sharing food is an international symbol of friendship, trust, respect, inlcusion and community. It is at the heart of all human relationships.

It gives grave offence for a community to banquet together behind closed doors or excluding boundaries of belief and practice. We can eat but you can only watch…

It enshrines at the heart of a faith community the power to exclude and to bestow or withhold favour and advantage. It teaches experientially discriminatory attitudes and a hierarchical approach to others.

Instead, we need to be bold in asserting that all food is the medium by which we express, seek and establish communion. We need no church, priest, confirmation, ritual, wafer or wine. A biscuit, a burger, or a bun. Pepsi, Tango or plain old water. A vindaloo or a fajita are far better at achieving holy communion than any church service could ever do.

Chapter 12

Tough Talk about Worship

Religious worship is covered rarely by the media. In England it remains the habit of the few and differs widely with most of the congregations in decline.

This situation that proves alarming to the churches is welcomed by the majority who see little value or purpose in praising God.

What's the point?

The primary issue is whether what happens in a church service has anything to do with God's wishes?

No is my unequivocal response.

If God exists, he/she would not require incessant adulation, gratitude and contrition. Such displays of servitude and obeisance are demeaning. Their concept arises from patriarchy and oligarchy and they abrade our understanding of relationship and authority.

Every aspect of what takes place in a church during worship is the sum total of a choreographed, scripted and performed community experience using various experiential mediums. It has no more or less to do with God than everything else that is presented similarly as a public artistic expression using words, music and movement.

Whether it has merit or otherwise from a human perspective is for us as critics to assess, but predominantly it fails to reach a reasonable standard.

The music

The experience of community singing is fun and can be exhilarating but it depends on the songs, the music and the lyrics.

Hymns and religious choruses appeal to a narrow band of society who is either from an older generation or who has been raised within those remaining rareified establishments which still practice daily worship. These are normally centres of privilege such as public schools, colleges or cathedrals.

The majority has no association or experience of what takes place musically within a church. Encountering it, most find it to be dull and repetitive and the lyrics superficial and pointless.

Even when a church experiments with modern music, it reproduces the uninspiring and mawkish sentiments directed towards God that mean nothing to the enligh*te*ned thinker.

The readings

Extracts from the Bible are read.

Although these are carefully chosen, they often hold little relevance and contain toxic elements. Despite the wealth and breadth of literature available in the world, much of which surpasses the Bible in profundity and beauty, congregations are forced to suffer a cyclical reading of biblical scripts.

Additional irritants are the use often of exclusive language and the meaningless declaration at the end of the reading that the words read are from the Lord, even when it is apparent they are not.

The sermon

It is astonishing that certain adults remain willing to subject themselves to the random musings of a preacher at every service, particularly when the poor delivery and insubstantial nature of the content makes it an exercise in patience.

When a charismatic or powerful preacher awes their audience, we should be even more suspicious. Such techniques have been used to inspire genocide.

Sermons maintain the patronising religious approach that the church is able to instruct the unenlightened in the ways of the divine. In educated societies, it is the church that often requires educating to relinquish magical thinking and embrace reality.

Radio 4's 'Thought for the Day' is an awkward and unwelcome intrusion each day into the thoughtful and complex analysis of current affairs. The act of daily worship has been moved but Sunday worship remains. Listening to it may provide nostalgic comfort for the older generation but for the rest, its self-righteous manner and hypocritical petitions are objectionable to the rest.

Producers need to be clear headed and move all such broadcasting on to a religious channel.

The community

Some are willing to suffer the above to gain the benefit of belonging. They feel secure wrapped around by others, by the 'church family' and by God. It makes the world less anonymous and their lives less pointless.

It is a retrograde choice though to stifle these burning and universal issues in the sterile environment of worship and deceive oneself that they have been satisfied.

The congregation participates in a ritualised relationship of intimacy with each other and with God, finding it hard to achieve either in reality.

Instead of communicating naturally together they manage their interaction, formalising it as Holy Communion. This involves them sitting beside one another but facing forwards, often bearing ill-will or resentment towards each other. They share a script. One person speaks and there is no chance to respond. They eat and drink in small measure and then leave.

There may be a chance for contact over coffee after the service, but this is brief, often in uncomfortable surroundings and an unsatisfactory way of building close friendships.

All this is based on adherence to the rules of the community which may be liberal or rigid but which set the relationships within an expectation of conformity, the breaking of which results in expulsion and rejection.

The giving

An integral part of each service is the collection when each worshipper is invited to donate towards the costs of the church. At times there are two collections within the same service.

The importance of promoting attendance becomes apparent. The organisation depends heavily on the regular giving of members. Persuading believers that worship is a required part of Christian devotion arises from the practical necessity of ensuring a source of income.

Would people still choose to go to church if they understood that God would rather they carried on with their lives and the only explanation for the practice is denominational fundraising?

Particularly when many children are deprived of the chance of a Sunday relaxing or exploring with their parents, who they may have seen only sporadically during the week, passed from nursery to child minder to creche to school. Many couples are denied quality time together, **after** hectic working weeks, to protect their love and build their home. Many sports people are kept from their competitions and many life opportunities and countless hours are wasted on a pointless exercise.

Rigor Mortis

The main denominations are frightened of life and inexperienced in spirituality. Their worship is rigid, following set liturgies or established protocols.

There is little room for experimentation and exploration.

The language that is used to address God and the culture and content of a service are kept within tightly controlled boundaries with clerics maintaining strict discipline.

God would have to be limited in expectation and intelligence, if what is on offer, decade after decade, proved in any way satisfying. Perceiving worship from a Divine perspective makes a mockery of it all.

What sort of a being would or could be satisfied by millions of subjects going through such Sunday rituals?

It beggars belief that if God is God, any of our earthly attempts at worship, are seen as anything but the vain pandering to our need to feel we have mystery and God under control. Worship is the most pretentious example of corporate delusional behaviour.

Assemblies

Few schools hold religious assemblies. Secular education cannot accommodate traditional religious practices and so children find they have little exposure to the realm and resources of spirituality.

In contrast, religious schools continue to entrap young minds with dogmatic belief and worship. Having chosen not only to accommodate but encourage Christian denominations to become responsible for schools, the government has been forced to permit the schools of other faiths also.

Rules requiring pupils to adhere to strict guidelines regarding uniform and customs both during school hours and beyond have profiled for us the shocking invasion and control over children's lives that can be meted out by religions, even in our own country. We find ourselves powerless to intervene because the trump card of faith has been played against us.

Schools must be secularised entirely, providing a safe and neutral environment within which children can thrive.

However, this doesn't mean they have to become spirituality jejune. They can still explore, in corporate settings, unaligned experiences of meditation, silence, contemplation, the use of candles, light and darkness, colours and movement, exercise and posture, music and the use of sound and tone to familiarise the child with resources by which they can begin to chart the inner and outer world where mysteries can be plumbed and the course of their life reviewed.

Chapter 13

Tough Talk about Religion

Religion has become a toxic influence internationally. It is embarrassing to be associated with something that has had and is having such a devastating effect. Some point to the many good people whose faith has motivated them to give their lives in the service of others, performing charitable and humanitarian work. Unfortunately although this may be true, there is often a price to pay.

As their incentive arises from a dogmatic source, their involvement is compromised by vested interests. They bear with them a faith and a culture that may be aggressively or implicity expressed. They are not innocent oases of love and altruism; rather they carry an agenda which will rise to every opportunity to deliver its underlying purpose, which is to proselytize.

The effects of this can sow division within families, communities and the society at large. The *r*eligious worker appears insensible to the bloody history that precedes them for which their faith is culpable.

Does the positive spin-off from their work counteract the wrongs and abuses of their religion?

A metanarrative

It is apparent that the multitudinous myths, legends, beliefs and religions spawned across the world form a convoluted history of a species in search of meaning and purpose.

Inasmuch as they harnassed meaning for a particular age and have contributed towards civilisation, they may have proved useful. The present situation is quite different. Their positive value appears minimal, their negative impact considerable and their role largely obsolete.

The fact that faith motivates one person to kill and another to nurse is no comfort to a modern age. We require a metanarrative that propels us beyond this primitive mode of direction, to one rooted in knowledge, human rights and responsibilities.

How do we escape the all pervading influence of religious thinking particularly if, as some claim, we are born predisposed towards belief?

The flight from childhood

The physical and pscho-social developmental stages involved in maturation show the complex journey into adulthood, contingent throughout on the oft repeated questions 'why – what – when – how – who'.

Our species, as the most intelligent *life* form known, uses these linguistic tools to accumulate knowledge.

They arise out of the pre-language experience of our ancestors, leading them to the assumption that nothing exists without a cause.

In the absence of information, enquiring minds speculated, using existing facts to try and work out the cause of an effect. When there were no human contenders, then the animals, the trees, the weather, the sun, the moon, the stars, spirits, gods, godesses were latched upon. Our memes, from primitive humans to the present day are laden with habits, customs, rituals and festivals arising from wild superstitions and religious speculations of every variety.

A child's eyes grow wide at the talk of Santa Claus, the tooth fairy and the Easter bunny. They are petrified at the idea of ghosts and gremlins. They imagine readily monsters under their beds and witches at the end of their gardens. They easily learn the religious language and belief of their family, culture and school. Fact, fiction and fantasy are all a part of the same world.

However, we all have to grow up.

Re-assessment

We can all remember the moments of enlightment in our lives, when we discard our previous assumptions and errant conclusions.

We no longer hang up stockings on Christmas Eve or place teeth under our pillows and most of us don't worry too much about mythical monsters. Yet we are less able to detach ourselves from our religious beliefs. This is in part a counterbalancing exercise to compensate for the childhood myths we have jettisoned and a refining of what is on offer; no longer an annual sleigh but an ever present generous God handling our requests every moment.

However, the fact that God doesn't deliver on his/her promises and that the practice of religion is more often a malignant force indicates that something more fundamental is involved.

We are pathologically incapable of handling the unknown and are adept at serial deception to maintain our pretence.

Distraction and dependency

Our species thoughout time has developed many techniques for avoiding or mitigating the uncomfortable.

Whether developing material dependencies such as wealth, posessions, alcohol, drugs, sex or relational dependencies expressed in continual social interactions or recreational dependencies absorbing us in sport, music, hobbies, culture and leisure – whatever our route, our aim is to find fulfillment and happiness.

Death, illness, mortality, origins, destination, the universe, the multiverse, the unknown are all frightening forces that threaten our equilibrium and peace. We don't have the facts to appease our questioning minds and still, in our century are thrown back upon that murky speculative world upon which religion is based.

Horrific religion

When we read about some of the horrific deeds carried out in the past in the name of religion we are appaulled and incredulous. We have learnt to sanitise our own version of religion so that it colour coordinates with our life design. Our belief is sweet and our worship inoffensive.

Christians seem affronted when you point out that they are drinking the blood of a man and eating his flesh. They are immune to how offensive it is that only the faithful few can share this holy food and most are excluded. They overlook the billions that are condemned to hell within their belief system. The acute agony of the majority that God ignores raises not an eyebrow.

Around the world Christians beat themselves, cut themselves, are crucified voluntarily and are rushed to hospital with severe blood loss, but none of this has the power to dent our fauning adoption of a sentimental christian belief.

Around the necks of many hangs a glinting gold cross, sometimes jewel encrusted. In the main, it does not represent a practiced allegiance to the Jesus faith, but rather it's a fashion accesory, a superstitious talisman, an unthinking appeasment to the God of childhood or an insurance policy against misfortune ahead.

When religious leaders jump on the back of this spineless wearing of the cross to try and deceive the public into the strength of the Christian faith today, they prevent an honest discussion taking place about people's disenchantment and rejection of traditional religious belief.

Beware the wolves

It is remarkable how intelligent, educated and rational human beings at the forefront of their intellectual disciplines can remain naive in their beliefs.

When challenged to describe the meaning of the religious words they use or the worship rituals they share, they abandon an analytical approach ring-fencing God with protective caveats such as – it's a matter of faith – the human mind can't comprehend.

It is clear that the fragility of the human psyche in the face of mystery is so all-pervading that even the greatest minds remain susceptible.

So, in our society, we have many leaders who appear erudite and whose espousal of religious faith attracts respect. They only have to speak and in the words of one religious journalist, Ruth Gledhill referring to Archbishop Rowan Williams can have a 'life-changing' effect on their audience.

I became shy of such displays long ago, when I realised that Hitler did too and so do many other tyrants and misleading orators. Human beings are terrifyingly maleable. Any unscrupulous preacher can benefit from people's raw human need. There is a surfeit of evidence of those brought under the spell of religious extremism who have been plucked from apparent normality to don suicide vests in the pursuit of religious devotion.

British Madrasahs?

The Madrasahs in Muslim countries are regarded with suspicion in the West. Rows of pupils memorising the Quran send shivers down our spines. Such schools are regarded as hotbeds of extremism where impressionable minds are enjoined to adopt a religious perspective.

However, Christian leaders have urged the government to ensure that religious education in UK schools is maintained.

Religions have evolved to provide a bulwark against the unkown. They are flawed speculations that resist progress, counter knowledge and encourage prejudice. The teaching of religion should be replaced by anthropology, psychology and sociology.

We must protect young minds from being hijacked by

religious thinking and root them firmly in a knowledge-based appraisal of the world.

Films and novels – Our modern Bible

Cultures have preserved their communal knowledge by enshrining them in folklore, superstitions, religious and secular mythology, about which students still learn.

The perspectives they contain may be irrelevant or timeless but the stories within which they are set are so timebound as to render them ineffective.

The same themes are woven into every book and every film that form a potent and pervading commentary on our world view. Education would be enhanced if this rich seam of cultural innovation could form an integral part of the curriculum. Instead of pouring over ancient texts and yesterday's answers we should assert our own prerogative to identify and explore the essential questions about life and arrive at our own considered answers

There is more resource for challenge, rebuke, inspiration and learning in a film such as 'The Hunger Games' than in any book of the Bible.

The pathological nature of religion

Can religions be benign?

Have they enabled otherwise dysfunctional or poorly performing individuals, groups or societies to be enhanced?

The evidence suggests that while religions can provide initially a cohesive structure to channel and direct human energy and aspiration, they all arrive at a point where their influence is debilitating.

At the heart of this pathology lies deceit. The establishment of purpose, principle and priorty on the basis of fiction purporting to be fact.

Once the masquerade is revealed, what can endure? Strip human history and experience of religion and what remains?

Have we achieved so much on the basis of a lie? Does so little remain on the basis of truth?

Yet truth is the only option

It alone can rescue us from the degenerative cycle of bloodshed and corruption that religion spawns and sustains.

While religious expressions form part of the universal human experience, each society must become inviolable to their subjective influence and must ensure that the instruments of public life including education, health and national occasions, such as commemorations and festivals use only inclusive and non-religious material.

Chapter 14

Tough Talk about Tomorrow's World

Human beings tend to nest into their environment, their culture and their age. Few are explorers willing to voyage beyond and think expansively. Familiarity with the known and fear of the unknown are adequate boundary setters.

It is breathtaking however to ponder the changes that a person living during the last hundred years has experienced. The modern advanced world is radically altered. Those who have resisted change have been left in a time warp. More encouraging are those who have kept abreast of the times and developments, such as ninety-year-olds facebooking, texting and skyping.

The question that lingers is what will tomorrow's world be like. What questions will be facing us in a hundred years and beyond and what spiritual and mental resources will be of use to us.

I suggest we will find ourselves placed in the traditional place of God.

Life

I predict that in the future we will become responsible for life itself.

Not only will we be able to choose the gender of our children, but their characteristics also. We will be faced with the complexity of creating a system that apportions freedom of choice to parents while retaining the required balance of difference within society.

We will be able to assess the optimum number of births that this planet can adequately sustain and will face the political challenge of creating a system that manages the equitable distribution of all resources.

We will also be able to design and generate new life and new life forms.

We will be able to integrate cellular, electronic and mechanical components into increasingly complex and functional cyborgs and humanoids.

We will be able to transfer a human's brain data, their 'consciousness', into artificial life forms or data banks and access them at will. The most intelligent minds of researchers, inventors and creators will continue to be available for consultations and commentary.

Dead loved ones could remain with us as apps on our smartphones.

We will be able to colonise other planets.

The evolution of life will be under our control.

Death

We will be able to extend life expectancy and halt the ageing process thus providing the physical possibility of eternal life.

As our planet will not be able to accommodate a burgeoning population, we will have to devise a system that apportions to every person a given lifespan with provision for them to arrange their 'ending of life' experience.

Healthy people will be able to choose between various methods of terminating their lives in a controlled, pain-free and pleasant environment.

Specialist centres will open offering an aesthetically uplifting and comforting setting for the departure of loved ones.

Religion

As economic development spreads across the globe and the benefits of education, health and prosperity encompass the entire population, as well as advances in scientific knowledge, so religious allegiances will fade.

In religion's place will come a curious respect for what we do not know and a maturity not to fill that gap with fairy tales and superstition.

Humility is always appropriate in the face of a lack of knowledge balanced with confidence in that which has been achieved and is known. However, future generations will be reticent to delude themselves with speculations that have no basis in fact or science.

A rigorous regard to present knowledge, personal responsibility and international governance will replace the present dependence on deities and religious authorities.

Morality

Recourse will not be made to divine entities and religious writings to justify altruistic and ethical behaviour but the rationale provided by inter-dependency and the necessity to achieve international co-operation rather than annihilation.

Once we have matured into the common view that the default position must be that we are responsible and there are no divine safety nets, then the mandate to aspire to an international commitment to promote equality, justice and peace for all will be realised.

Subservient obedience to a commander will be replaced by a common espousal of agreed values for sought after ends.

There will be no room for jingoistic attitudes or isolationist practices. Governance will be slow and somewhat tedious, the product of deliberation and debate.

Cohesion will arise from a balance of power being maintained between the world's multitudinous groups.

The alternative

With warnings of environmental catastrophe, the present ideological, religious, economic and cultural impasses and persistent criminality it may be that having reached the edges of such possibilities we are prevented from going further.

Perhaps entire civilisations will disappear. All advanced life forms on earth could be eradicated. Our globe, wiped clean, may have to start the evolutionary process all over again.

The entire system of ordered energy may be so fundamentally disordered that it is swallowed up in some ultimate black hole awaiting a subsequent 'big bang'.

Billions of years may have to pass before a new species, comparable to humanity, but perhaps quite distinct, will have its own chance to journey further and solve the conundrums about which I have written.

What is certain is that development depends upon knowledge. Its accumulation will lead us from dumb foragers to the dispensers of life and death and the architects of our future well-being or destruction.

The challenge

Before it is too late, we must find a new way that takes us beyond religion and yet satisfies our religious needs.

When faced with new frontiers, the faith lobby are often those who opine negatively, urging caution, laying down ethical obstacles and preventing a wholehearted commitment to research. The boundaries set by one generation are breached by the next as the tides of enquiry and knowledge lap ever higher.

The restrictions people have set are subjective representations of the lack of imagination, courage and willingness to embrace the unknown. God is the usual excuse given and the foundation built upon to make such diffidence respectable.

Whereas in the earlier stages of civilisation the price of delay was limited, now with the technological possibilities brimming and an immense array of opportunities emerging, there is no shuffle room. Now is the time for us to take responsibility.

But how?

Part III

Chapter 15

A Journey towards the Light

Having looked afresh at religion we begin to realise that we had been tricked and trapped. We had been immersed in a faith and spoon-fed with its language, culture and beliefs in such a comprehensive way that it had been impossible for us to evaluate it clearly and objectively.

This book offers us, hopefully, a key for our release.

As we have been incarcerated since childhood we may well fear this newfound freedom. The opening of our cell door may come as a shock, even an offence to us. We are likely to find ourselves resisting determinedly the invitation to step beyond what is familiar.

We can begin to berate and despise this liberating approach and at worst want to slaughter the one that bears it, as has happened in numerous cultures.

If you find yourself nervous of being challenged and changed, perhaps you shouldn't read further. You can return at any time to your habitual ways, beliefs and certainties.

On the other hand, we could be brave. If we are adventurers and truth seekers, we have nothing to fear.

Fortitude

We may well encounter numerous moments as we try and apply this new understanding, when we find we want to *with*draw; when what is familiar to us offers us the promise of comfort in contrast to alien territory.

We may experience disturbing reactions. Our dreams may be unsettled. Anxiety may plague us and that may trigger physical, mental or emotional consequences.

However, all this in time will prove worthwhile as we

withdraw from the lies, sweet stories and the **m**yth**s** that have confused us since childhood.

Preliminary requirements and observations

First, it may help if we discover the process by which we were captured in the beginning. This will reveal how deep the foundations were sunk, in reality beyond our reach or our memory.

As babies we were greeted by a myriad of intense sensory experiences. Colours, shapes, noises, tastes, smells and movements abounded.

Our response to them was to make a variety of unrecognisable sounds. Then emerging from the cacophony around us, certain sounds became distinct and we began to associate them with form, movement and experience:

For instance... Ibu... (if we are Malay) or Mum (if English)...

...Apu... (if Hungarian) or Dad (if English)

Copying

At a certain point we developed the ability to mimic these sounds and to experience the approval for doing so by the adults around us.

As a toddler we started to cruise, to grip onto solid objects and pull ourselves up. The adults around us ide*n*tified what we were holding onto for us as:

...Maca... (if Macedonian) or Table (if English)

So far the association of sounds to objects was based on our physical experience and as we have shown, across the world, each language associated different sounds to the same objects.

It is important to grasp the fact that the allocated sound was merely a signpost guiding us to something else. We learned easily those sounds that linked to something important, constant and identifiable, like Dad, Mum, table, car, doll.

The invisible zones

However, other sounds were being used which pointed less clearly to what they described, to an invisible realm of – good and bad, nice and nasty, right and wrong etc. We learned that these sounds expressed value and approval or their opposite and they complicated our learning experience by becoming attached or associated to the other sounds.

Boys may have played with dolls and heard frowning adults commenting that dolls were for girls. The two sounds, dolls and girls, became linked and a value attached itself of disapproval for a boy to play with them.

Additionally, at a certain point in our development, we encountered sound associations being made for another realm entirely.

Enter the Divine

...Boh... (if Slovakian)...Jum*a*l... (if Estonian)...Zot (if Albanian) or God (if English);

And value sounds were attached to these also.

What becomes chilling is the realisation that the complex linguistic code by which we communicate and transact our lives is not as simple as we thought. It is soaked in the values of others.

Others have not only named our world and experiences but interpreted them.

Before we had a chance to make our own sense of life, it was already being packaged and delivered to us. Unaware of this, we matured believing we were in control, overlaying these early experiences with what appeared to be our own language and values. However, on closer inspection we were building on the foundation laid by others and working to their design.

The task of identifying the foundations and assessing the design is frustrated by the fact that so much lies hidden beyond the reach of memory.

However, in glimpsing the problem we can set about trying to reclaim our desire to interpret our world.

Inspecting the foundations

Initially we need to loosen the foundations of all the words (sounds) that are significant in our lives.

We need to realise that they are secondary and interchangeable and have been given to us by others, according to the language code of our particular part of the world.

We need to spend time exploring what value sounds or experiences are associated with them.

For instance if we don't enjoy the experience of reading, we might find that sounds like 'waste of time', 'egg heads', 'boffins', 'boring' are attached to the sound and experiences of frowns, irritation and sarcasm.

When we discover, that a significant word has multiple value words, sounds such as tuts or gestures like frowns attached to it, similar to viruses that have corrupted files on our computer, we can choose to take action.

A new language

First, we can begin to experiment with replacing the offending word with our own original sound. It sounds silly, but can be fun.

For example, instead of the sound 'reading' we could use 'shammassing' or instead of the sound 'good' we could say 'vwulsg' or instead of the sound 'God' we could use 'Turfoosh'.

We can be playful in choosing different sounds and enjoy the various sensations that arise from creating our own personal value-free language for the first time in our lives.

However, the serious purpose is to identify words that have particular significance in our lives and are laden with 'value viruses' and to try and replace them with sounds that bring no other associations with them.

To kill for a word?

When we have loosened the signposts, appreciated that sounds are randomly applied, realised the value-laden nature of the words we use and when we have experimented with creating new sounds, we are ready to contemplate how preposterous it is to think we can blaspheme, by using a sound.

Saying 'G is evil' is fine.

Saying 'Go is evil' is fine.

Saying 'Od is evil' is fine.

Saying 'Fod is evil' is fine.

Saying 'Hod is evil' is fine.

Saying 'God is evil' is a blasphemy.

More curious still, saying 'Zot is *e*vil' is fine if you are English, but blasphemy if you are Albanian.

The innocence of language begins to fade. We are using other people's sounds and by using them we are implicated in other people's values, politics, power and vested interests.

No one will blink if we say 'Turfoosh' because it is pure, innocent, uncontaminated.

Is your table the same as my table?

The fact that we can be accused of blasphemy for 'mis-using' a sound and in many societies still be executed for doing so makes the exact meaning of a sound, in a particular context, paramount.

However, the mystery deepens when we consider that the exact meaning remains illusive. The hearers of a recognised sound may conjure up different images, because exactly what the sound, as a signpost, is pointing to is not defined in a precise manner. Each image will bring with it different associated value words.

The image/s that spring to mind when we hear the following words may well be different from someone else's, even though they may share a common theme.

Table – Car – Machine – Printer – Castle.

For instance, for 'car' we may think about a vehicle, but what image has our brain given us – a mini, a Rolls or a Noddy car; a red car, blue or yellow; on a road or a track; convertible, saloon or estate; taxi or police car?

The associated value words are very different if we are thinking of a Noddy car rather than a police car.

Abstract images

The more abstract the word becomes, the greater the variety of image/s.

Love – Generosity – Hope – Hatred.

If we hear the word 'Love', what image is triggered primarily? Is it a mother suckling her baby, or an aid worker distributing food, or two partners making love, or siblings holding hands?

Sometimes a conversation is fraught with hidden obstacles because the language used is spawning different images, whose value words are provocative.

If we argue that love is all that matters in the world because we are thinking about caring for the poor, we may well get into an argument with an aid worker who thinks mistakenly that we are saying that sex is our top priority. Such misunderstandings can be resolved without too much difficulty.

However, not so when metaphysical words are used.

God – Angels – Heaven

We have seen how the random sound 'God' points to that which is most precious for a believer and comes with multiple value associations that can prompt them to murder you. However, managing to establish what these are proves well nigh impossible.

In order not to cause offence, so much becomes ring-fenced that meaningful discussion fails. We are faced with the absurdity that the process of allocating sounds reaches an impasse where no sounds can be used at all. Communication ceases and the silence of fear reigns.

Even the images are not really our own

Unsettling again is the discovery that the pictures that flash up in our minds at the use of words are the random collection of experiences that the people and the world around us have provided.

Our images for machine will be different if we are a poor rural worker in India rather than a car factory worker in Germany.

Our images for love will be different if we come from a brutal abusive background rather than a child from a secure nurturing home.

Our images for God will be different if we have been brought up in North Korea or in Iran or in America.

Those who travel abroad for the first time or to new continents can often return thinking differently because they have been exposed to a new take on the same world.

In the same way that the sounds themselves and the values attached to them have been chosen by others, it begins to become apparent that many, even most of the images they produce do not belong to us either.

The signposts, the associated values and the images to which they point are all in various degrees given to us.

We are faced with the question of whether we can call any of these constructs our own?

Philosophical prisons

There are yet more invading influences.

Circling around us as we acquire language, associated values and images, are those who want to package our composite knowledge that forms our view of the world into a particular cultural, political, religious and philosophical form. The conditioning or programming we have thus far experienced is apparently insufficient. It provides the raw material for those we may call the 'macro-programmers'; those who are going to provide the operating system that will handle everything else, like our latest version of Windows or Apple Mac.

The interest groups they represent want to expand their base of influence and power and we are their targets.

As parasites feed off their host, so those who represent particular vested interests want to colonise our brief earthly lives for their own purposes.

Conforming captives

In the end we are captured, 'educated' and taught to conform.

We are given an identity, which we are ready and willing to defend, even to aggressively promote, even to die doing so. We are citizens of a particular country, members of a race, believers in a faith, activists in a political movement or interest group, promoters of a philosophy, wearers of a brand.

Further, we are subscribers to a cultural approach, an age bound system. In the UK, despite all our differences, we are 'controlled' by certain accepted institutions. We are informed by the media, entertained by theatre, screens and radio, governed by leaders and political parties, ordered by the police and disciplined by the courts.

We are obsessed with football primarily, but all sports have sporting heroes and celebrity heroes. We participate in mass events – the Olympics, reality TV shows, concerts and royal occasions. We are susceptible to advertising, branding and the latest fashions. We eat mass-produced foods from global companies. We eat, drink, wear, read, watch and spray on what we are told by those with the money to tell us.

We are subject to so many influences that much of our lives, in the end, belong to someone else.

We have been colonised and cloned, brainwashed, yet made to think we are free.

We must be shaken into an awareness of this.

Our language, our images and our identity may all belong to others.

Welcome to the first day of our lives

Let's be resolute.

We must climb out of our present identity. Shed our skins. Scan our minds. Set aside our beliefs. Shake the foundations of our language. We must become naked, as those newly born.

We must step away from our language, culture, country, community, philosophy and first language.

We must begin to look, listen, taste, touch, feel, experience and describe all things as new, within ourselves and without.

We must move to the very edge, peer into the mystery and ask ourselves what, why, where, who…

Remember though, we are naked and vulnerable, as newborns. We must watch out and be cautious. There are hordes gathering and encircling us, detecting opportunity, speculating, sniffing out virgin ground. They come to offer us their packages of answers…

'Zot made the world… become a socialist… take out a subscription to OK magazine… worship Jumal… drink Bacardi… sniff cocaine… try Reiki healing… get hooked on Eastenders… Boh requires your obedience… join the Kylie fan club… what star sign are you?… Christ is calling to your heart… God loves you…'

We must keep them all at arm's length, particularly those that appear familiar and promise comfort.

Stairway to heaven

The climb ahead of us is steep and tortuous.

How do we unlearn or vacate our minds of what we have been told. How do we rid ourselves of associative memories?

An interesting illustration of the challenge involved in

separating ourselves from what we have heard, involves the Led Zeppelin song 'Stairway to Heaven'. In 1982 it was claimed that a technique called 'backward masking' had been used during recording.

You can hear this for yourself on the Internet. The relevant site allows you first to listen to the particular lyrics of the song played normally:

Then you can listen to the same lyrics played in reverse.

In reverse you will hear a cacophony of sounds that make no sense at all.

However, when you listen to them in reverse again while you read the following hidden message it is said to contain, you will hear:

Oh here's to my sweet Satan.

The one whose little path would make me sad,

whose power is Satan.

He will give those with him 666.

There was a little tool shed where he made us suffer, sad Satan.

Repeat this a few times and you will find that each time you play it, the words become ever clearer, until you can't imagine how you missed it at first.

Further, when you know the above text, it becomes impossible not to hear it anymore.

Escaping the programming

The realisation that our minds are thoroughly and comprehensively imprinted in a similar manner by everything that we have heard, seen and experienced makes our quest to name, identify, apportion value and think originally extremely hard.

Recent research and experiments illustrating the limitations of the human brain and its vulnerability to manipulation are sobering. You only have to watch Derren Brown to see how we can be taken over completely by another. It seems that many of the mental processes that give us our feelings, values, preferences and lead us to make decisions are beyond our awareness or analysis. It seems we know so little about ourselves.

All these things should stir a degree of anger or irritation at what others have done to us or are doing to us that can fuel, hopefully, a burgeoning curiosity about what we can make of the world if we approach it anew and with a questioning intent. If we are in charge and we are responsible.

Chapter 16

Poisonous models

First though, we must try and analyse the macro-programme and the values that created it and have up to now controlled us.

1. Leadership

Where does our fixation with being led originate? Is it the perpetuation of the rule of the animal kingdom, that the strongest, most powerful, most canny, most camouflaged, most attractive, most everything wins through?

It seems that brute strength and its many derivatives claim precedence over our lives?

It seems we have developed the legends, myths, fairy stories and religious dogmas that will help underpin this primitive driving force of achieving status and precedence through competitive success.

The lesson we learn and continue to convey is that there must always be a hierarchy culminating in a leader. There must always be a competition producing a winner. There must always be struggles from which heroes emerge.

Rewards

From those who start a race, someone will cross the finishing line first. One might have thought that this fact alone was satisfaction enough. The fact has been noted that a particular person has been identified as the fastest runner, or swimmer, or hurdler etc.

However, in deference to the macro-programme, we shower the winner with accolades; medals, money, fame, adulation and iconic status. They appear on hoardings all over the country and on TV adverts. They receive further attention with 'personality of the year' awards or 'sportswoman or man of the year' awards.

Rebecca Adlington, the British swimmer who won gold medals in 2008 and bronze medals in 2012, has revealed that the attention she received after the Beijing Olympics forced her into therapy.

The successful become the means by which large companies market their products and enjoin us as branded followers.

This craving within us to make winners is indulged with vote-based reality TV, where on the X Factor, Britain's Got Talent, I'm a Celebrity – Get me out of here, Strictly Come Dancing etc. we are encouraged to create our next idol.

Even in the dry and cynical world of politics we are coerced into an increasingly meaningless system where fat budgets, paying for clever spin and savvy makeovers, turn our politicians into people we support with little reference to their actual policies or intentions.

At the heart of the system exists the royal family, as our ultimate paradigm. Stripped of executive authority, existing solely to represent our inherent longing to have representative figures through whom we can live vicariously.

Wherever we look, the model plays itself out. In the Board room, in the Council Chamber, in the Supreme Court; in the Churches, Synagogues and Temples; in the local community groups, bowls teams and pubs; in the groups of friends to which you belong, the 'leader' is bestowed or bestows him or herself with special powers and graces.

The devastating consequences

If it is so prevalent, then shouldn't it be accepted as an inherent trait and need of humanity?

We have many impulses and passions however, that we curb as civilised people. It is not an acceptable argument for a person to claim that natural urges led him or her to sexually abuse or murder.

In contrast we have sanitised our urge to appoint leaders and to be led.

It might not be of concern, if it caused no harm. Evidence suggests the contrary. Everything we invest in another as our 'leader, hero, and celebrity' we denude from ourselves.

Our attention is taken up reading about, watching, considering and reacting to the lives and choices of others instead of our own.

Our interest is in the development of someone else's career, singing, sporting skills and political choices rather than our own.

Our belie*f* is that these others deserve our attention because they are 'more' in some way than we are. Their love life is more riveting than our own. Their marriage is more important than our own. Their baby's birth is more life-changing than our own.

It's a trick born of the macro-programme that robs us of our lives and our happiness.

It would seem risible if we asked a friend to come and photograph us at home, in the various rooms of our house, changing into different outfits and then had them published in a magazine to be sold. Yet this is what happens in so many glossy magazines. Worse still, we support the idea and even pay for it. What we would regard as ludicr**ou**s for us we pay for and flag up as fine for others. After all, we muse, their lives are 'more…' than ours.

The brain and skill drain

By diverting attention away from our own lives, we neglect the unique experiment that each of us comprises.

Every moment spent gazing at other people's lives and finding magic or amazement through them should be spent honing our personal skills and increasing our ability to contribute positively in our own situations.

Perhaps you are a nurse transfixed by the cavorting of an X Factor contestant and allured by the superficial comment by one of the judges that the performer doesn't ever have to go back to their old job. Instead, you should recognise that loving and caring for another is of supreme importance and the challenge is not to pine after fame but to long to love and care for your patients ever more sensitively.

Perhaps you are a refuse collector transfixed by a football star scoring an astonishing goal and allured by their excessive income. Instead, you should realise the immense public service you perform maintaining public health and order and taking pride in handling each day's work at maximum efficiency.

Perhaps you are a checkout worker transfixed by the Duchess of Cambridge, allured by a lifestyle of designer clothes and jewelled royalty. Instead you should realise the amount of people that you meet each day and the unique opportunity you have to lift their spirits and make them feel better.

The truth is that in a civilised society we no longer need or should want to pander to the leader macro-programme. We want to build together a community in which each person is regarded and treated as of equal value, where each person fulfils well their role in life and where no one is given undue attention or heaped with excessive praise or exposed to disproportionate scrutiny or paid infla*te*d salaries and extortionate bonuses, all of which distort the balance we are trying to establish.

People will buy the music they enjoy but they shouldn't be encouraged to obsess about the singer. We can applaud the winner of a race, but they shouldn't then become an advertising commodity. We can respect the selfless service of the Queen, but we shouldn't then believe that she is anyway 'above' us.

However, at the moment, the macro-programme coerces us into ever more fixated states of dependence, spawning a constant stream of leader/hero figures. It may be an apparently more benign form of mass control than that seen in North Korea but it still subjugates us to a primitive form of functioning from which it is imperative we evolve.

2. By what authority?

As humanity panders to its need for a leader, so we are conditioned to assume that we must be given authority in order to function effectively.

Who or what gives me the right?

We are all required to live within the law, but we clutter our lives and restrict our freedom by submitting ourselves to extra layers of authority and regulation.

We may follow the Bible as the Word of God containing, we say, God's laws, or another selected holy book. We may have a Guru or spiritual guide. We may follow a dietary plan or a health programme. We may choose to live 'environmentally', 'frugally' or 'politically'. We may be a Mason, a Soroptimist, a Rotarian or a member of the Women's Institute. We have many ways of shackling ourselves to further codes of conduct and by so doing; it seems to provide legitimacy for our actions, choices and pastimes.

When challenged, with confidence, we refer the enquirer to the source of our authority. 'It says in the Bible... Environmentalists think... As a Mason...' Somehow it makes us feel inadequate and unauthorised just to say, 'Well I chose...' It is as though we had no permission to choose anything ourselves.

We have allowed our birthright, our own authority, to be usurped.

And who is responsible?

There is another disadvantage to leader figures receiving our adulation. In our increasingly litigious society we pursue zealously lines of responsibility to reach the one who will bear the penalty when things go awry.

As we love to adore our idols and require leaders throughout society, we delight too in their demise and gloat over their disasters or failings. We allow others to bask in public glory while fantasising about taking their place; but then we collude in the process of heaping shame upon them, out of our sublimated irritation.

We think that by staying out of the limelight we don't have to choose and so won't get into trouble for any mistakes made. We don't realise that the cost is to render our lives insignificant.

Growing up

In childhood, authority always belonged to others; our parents, teachers and the adult world. Maturation should have allowed us to transition into bearing authority ourselves, unless during those years, language was suffused with values that would impede our growth.

If the adults who raised us, while bearing authority, attached to it the value that it was derived from elsewhere, from a divine entity, moral code, sacred writing, law book etc., then the experience of bearing authority ourselves would precipitate two responses, either to look for its origin as a subservient or to claim to be the origin as a despot.

What is missing is the reality that each of us has personal authority, and only by using this aright, in conjunction and co-ordination with others, can all authority find its proper expression.

3. Big is to be trusted

The grain of sand is of importance only because, with all the others, it helps constitute a beach.

Alone, we are nothing...

Notable, however, is the fact that individual genius has brought such benefit to existence. So many scientific break-throughs, works of art and inventions are the work of individuals. There have been so many new movements, campaigns against oppression and injustice and donations towards innovative research that have originated with individuals.

There is, it seems, a cultural conflict between the individual, struggling to be spotted, to contribute and to survive and the greater power of the mass to decide who is going to gain attention. TV reality shows are an interesting example, as they purport to give people an equal chance before the mass. Everyone involved, nevertheless, is subject to varying degrees of group manipulation producing a final manufactured winner.

Often genius goes undetected perhaps for years, perhaps forever, because the luck, money, advertising, public interest doesn't pick it up. Its merit is not altered by this fact. It remains genius.

The question arises why the reaction of others remains so important for us? During our childhood years we were encouraged to perform and rewarded for it. Our learning was fostered by the acclaim we received for our achievement. We entered adulthood with this same carrot mentality, except by then it had been adulterated by the vested interests of popular culture and economics.

We had learned to please by conforming. Our choice of clothes, music, hairstyle, accent, shoes etc., all gave us a place amongst others, based on their positive reaction.

The power of the crowd was ascendant.

Layer upon layer

As society evolves, power circulates between groups, with each vying for precedence. It may appear that we are dealing with individuals; however, they are merely the face of the group. Ultimately, the individual, unless they are able to achieve autocracy, becomes powerless.

Whereas an individual can be scrutinised, holding an institution to account or the individuals within it proves more illusive. Everyone has a place to hide and a finger to point.

We could decide to trust only individuals that we respect and value that which has remained small and accountable, but our many needs drive us from this safer conclusion.

If the Roman Catholic Church says it, we can trust it. Then we discover decades of child abuse.

If the Chief Constables say it, we can trust it. Then we discover officers lying and fabricating evidence.

If the Appeal Court Judges says it, we can trust it. Then we discover chilling miscarriages of justice.

If the Newspapers say it, we can trust it. Then we discover covert hacking even to a dead girl's phone.

If the BBC says it, we can trust it. Then we discover shocking allegations that have been buried.

If the Prime Minister says it, we can trust it. Then we discover it was at best false and at worst a deliberate manipulation.

If the politician or the celebrity says it, we can trust it. Then we discover they were sexual abusers.

Will the penny drop?

Whatever is disclosed and however shocking the revelations are, does not seem to have the power to dislodge our misplaced loyalty. On announcing the latest scandal, the powers that be assure the public that an enquiry will be held, as if this will placate troubled minds. We appear calmed.

Why? A flawed group is now to be investigated by possibly another flawed group that will produce possibly another flawed report that will in time be exposed by possibly another flawed group etc. The two most recent examples of this are the handling of Bloody Sunday and the Hillsborough disaster.

It becomes apparent that at times corporate life reduces efficiency, dulls creativity and induces corruption.

4. Democracy

Democracy appears to be the secular religion. It is presented as the gospel for the world and the answer to every nation's ills.

The idea that each of us has a vote because our opinion is

important and by expressing it we can shape and change our world is a beguiling one.

Evolution pits us in direct and aggressive competition with the world around us. We must survive against all odds. Progress relies upon a ruthless individualism that uses community only inasmuch as it enhances the prospects for survival.

The apparent companionability and cosiness of human unity masks a terrible truth, that its components are all evolutionary enemies. Present alliances are expedient and transitory. Lurking and ready to emerge is the beast.

Group dynamics hint at this reality.

An analysis of political decision-making and voting patterns exposes the influence that money, big business, advertising and spin exert upon the electorate who as pawns are played cynically by the power brokers.

Strong nations, conglomerates and individuals use community to satisfy their vested interests and democracy is a convenient method of camouflaging their practices.

A political M-theory

As science tries to grapple with the concept of a fundamental theory that can accommodate many realities at once, even when in conflict, so must our political understanding.

Espousing democracy alone is doomed to failure.

Individuals and communities can never be safe when subject to a majority, particularly when coercive, yet imperceptible forces prey upon that m*a*jority.

There has to be a finely achieved equilibrium between the rights of the individual and the group. How this is achieved will depend on each context, different in China, the UK, Saudi Arabia and India etc. What is paramount is protecting the conversation that must occur freely between all involved.

5. Magic, religion and superstitions are OK

Perhaps these are the most poisonous models of all.

They have swallowed up so much human time and resource, destroyed so many lives, wreaked havoc between families, communities and nations and spawned the pseudo-science of theological and paranormal academic exploration.

When shown to be bogus and non-existent, the enormity of the waste is fully appreciated.

Liberal religionists

Even those who take the broadest most modern view are still unwittingly caught in a web of deception as they try and make sense of redundant dogmas. Their quest to reinvigorate people's views of religion satisfies the macro-programming that won't permit them to expunge religion from their lives.

If one urges people to move from a literal to a metaphorical view of religious or paranormal language, one maintains their link to the debilitating fantasies that halt their maturation.

It induces a form of narcotic delirium by detaching people from the world and realities around them and inducing them to maintain the myth of a thought and word-based existence more potent than that which is known.

6. Get your proper share of sex, drugs, food and alcohol

'Fifty Shades of Grey' has sold over 65 million copies worldwide. The developed world surrounds itself with sexual imagery that becomes ever more provocative, invasive, disturbed and explicit.

Marriages and primary relationships suffer intense external pressures that erode and fracture them invariably.

Even the boundaries of childhood are being assaulted by marketing brands, glossy magazines, kids' TV programming and advertising and their exposure to the Internet through smart-phones and a plethora of electronic devices.

Talk of girlfriends and boyfriends begins at reception, fashion wear becomes of note at kiddies' discos and messaging allows content in conversations that is unsupervised and damagingly excessive.

Substance dependent

Affluent societies are deluged with consumer goods, the sale of which buoys the economy. We are tempted, cajoled, coerced and finally conned into purchasing. Our consumer economy encourages us into addiction.

Happiness is portrayed in terms of possessions, and monetary power.

Those with few resources often become ensnared by alcohol and food, developing obesity and alcoholism.

Those with more resources chase bigger and better homes, cars, jewels, holidays.

Those with great resources add yachts, helicopters and jets to the 'I want' list, but they also, in their ennui and their disenchantment with excess, fall prey to hard drugs.

And everyone is vulnerable at any time to the casual offer of soft drugs or easy sex.

Are you missing out?

The macro-programme makes us feel neglected, cheated, and left out of the party if we are not at the forefront of the action.

'Ah it's sadism now – let's try it.'

'Are you sniffing – give me some.'

'Weekends are for bingeing.'

'Everyone sleeps around – don't you?'

7. Our obsession with being noticed

It seems that we are not able to contemplate an ordinary life as satisfactory. We have to attract attention in varying degrees, whether it drives us to audition for 'Britain's Got Talent' or the 'X factor' or simply to wear make-up or designer tops we are all caught at the same game.

It is as though we gain our existence or our credibility because others have observed us. The social machine is driven by this desire for recognition and we are adept at pandering to it in every way imaginable. Why?

Why do we obsess about others and want them to obsess about us? Other animals appear content to be about their own business. A cow isn't looking to check that they are on camera and a snail doesn't court headlines!

'Look at me Mum and Dad'

From infancy we have been looking for and encouraged to receive attention. Doting parents commenting on our actions and cooing over our achievements attune us to seek their pleasure and satisfy their hopes.

This reciprocal encouragement is vital perhaps to child-rearing but when overplayed it can produce attention dependent children that become insufferable adults.

Indulgent observation of children appears to be a scourge of wealthier nations. There is little time or inclination to be so occupied when faced with a daily battle for survival. Spoilt adults raise spoilt children.

Reality shows

TV akin to 'Big Brother' makes a nightmare of the process. A group of adults are watched 24/7 and are afforded no privacy. Their every move and conversation are analysed and interpreted by a voyeuristic public.

The film 'The Truman Show' parodied this. It imagined a child born and raised within an artificial world, generated and controlled by TV executives, of which he was unaware. Viewers from around the world tuned in daily to follow his life. As the truth of his situation begins to dawn on us, so it does on him and we share his desire to understand his contrived situation and see him escape from it.

God, our TV executive?

The distaste we feel is curious.

Is not the widespread belief in some form of God uncomfortably similar?

At its most sinister, the creator of all things, watching everything created, managing, controlling, predestining, intervening, guiding and planning the whole. We, aware of the divine 24/7 surveillance, direct our lives accordingly, paying relative amounts of deference or otherwise to the big eye in the sky. Whether we warm to the idea or detest it, it seems that the macro-programme has conditioned us to have to grapple with a basic inner drive to be watched and to watch, as well as being expected to perform.

It seems it is so hard to grow up and to arrive at a place where we are content to be, as the sheep nibbling grass or the bee alighting on pollen, unobserved, unexpected and at peace.

Gods to others

Our entrapment into a 24/7 cycle of observed behaviour is visited on the world around so that we all become a pair of prying eyes.

We have so much to say about the choices of those around us, the affairs of the world, the antics of celebrities, in fact any life or situation that captures our attention.

We love to set ourselves up as God, Judge, Sage, Agony Aunt/Uncle, Teacher, Counsellor etc. in order to solve the problems arrayed around us. We cannot let others be or give them the dignity of resolving their own dilemmas. We must add our commentary, publish our news reports and fill the airwaves with our solutions. We are responding to programming forces of which we are unaware, that sadly erode our freedom and our serenity.

All these models must go

If we are to wrest control from the macro-programme we must be truly original.

We are not looking at others. We do not want a leader. We are not going to be led. We will believe in ourselves. We will respect our personal authority to determine and decide. We will be cautious about corporations, groups and large organisations. We will not assume democracy is benign. We will protect the individual. We will not waste time on religion or allow ourselves to be allured into the cul-de-sac magic provides.

We will not allow advertising or the prevailing culture to set our agenda and make our choices. We will not become addicts nor be tricked into believing that becoming enveloped into the consumer economy will lead us to fulfilment. We will resist the need to be noticed, stop performing and divert our attention from the lives of others so that we can all be allowed just to be in peace.

Part IV

Chapter 17

A New Way of Believing

So, the world needs a fresh approach to religion and spirituality. We must adopt a new language to house our experience of mystery and rely upon modern concepts and stories to convey important truths.

Economic development and education have bred a proper scepticism towards the traditional religious packages, but they have not removed the underlying need for a relevant spirituality.

Many may not espouse a particular religious brand, but they are comfortable referring to loved ones being in heaven or continuing to exist in some undefined place or way. They pray or wish for luck when under duress and think that there may be some sort of being, energy, entity or 'God' somewhere.

Those who reject the God approach are still aware of mystery and the unanswered questions that tease and trouble us.

It is crazy that argument and bloodshed have resulted from religious divisions, when in reality every person shares a common humanity and the puzzlement that it occasions.

Now is the time to evolve our spiritual insights to remove the shackles of yesterday's dogmas while providing accessible resources for today.

The 'God' issue

In order to escape any contamination or association with the past or the present, I suggest we stop using the sound 'God' altogether and its linguistic equivalents and use a universal sound for what is unknown:

'MMMM'

You sound it just by humming the 'm' sound without opening your lips. Sounding it for too long tickles, so it is self-limiting to avoid zealous repetition.

Its sound expresses a thoughtful uncertainty, perhaps accompanied with a slight shrug of the shoulders.

The sound is pristine and untainted, emptied of the historical clutter and dogmatic baggage of ages past.

We must resist the urge to regard it as a receptacle into which we can pour our inanities and simplicities.

So of what purpose is this sound or indicator?

It represents the mystery of everything that we do not know or understand, especially those things that give value, purpose, succour and meaning to life.

It signifies our quest, search, longing and aspiration for understanding.

It establishes a neutral focus by which we can negotiate the realm of the known and the unknown.

It provides a screen onto which we can project our imaginings and have them scrutinised by others.

It recognises that every image or word we may use remains equivocal, a mere sketch, an impressionist's view with all its expected distortion and limitation.

Keeping the sound empty of fixed associations

The sound points to a screen that allows for an infinite variety of ideas and images to play before a person and the world. However, a strict policy should prevent anything being shown continually on the screen and so being associated permanently with the sound.

It is essential that the default state of the screen is to be blank.

The moment something is placed there permanently, however small, that part becomes the possession of the one who placed it and the ones who agree with its placement. They have colonised a portion of the mystery and the rot has begun.

The deposit creates a claim to ownership and the political

ramifications of the need to protect and to control their 'property rights'.

Every time someone else wishes to place a subsequent image that varies from the first, they require their own space, and in no time the screen is cluttered with multiple fixed images, each purporting to be an accurate representation of MMMM.

Conflict follows. War is not far behind.

Empty screens

The screen must stay empty, other than for the transitory images of everyone's speculations.

The sound 'MMMM' indicates that which we do not know and so can only imagine.

A simple matter of truth

It is incontestable to state that we have no objective evidence that proves the existence of God. Equally, there is no evidence that proves anything that has ever been claimed about God.

The holy books, spiritual tomes, sermons and religious claims are all speculation.

Beliefs, dogmas, doctrines and catechisms are all imagination and philosophy.

They are not facts and they are not science.

The sound MMMM, to be true, must remain empty.

Stop lying to the children

We do not want to corrupt the mind of a child or an adult by tricking them into believing that we know something about MMMM, when the truth is we don't.

We don't want to put fairy stories permanently onto the screen. We don't want to present fiction as fact. We don't think myths and legends have a constant place. We don't think Father or Mother Christmas or the elves should be screened perpetually.

We want to ensure that the screen is the place for ideas to be scrutinised, reviewed and criticised. Images to tantalise our imaginations, spur our creativity and spurn new speculative thinking, but all of it understood to be subjective and transitory.

But the critics have rated my film the best

So what happens when someone creates images that are popular. The crowd likes a particular representation of MMMM that someone has projected. They want it to keep showing.

It excites them and satisfies them. It accords with their philosophical understanding of life and existence. They want to brand it, market it and make it a global multinational film.

In the market place of ideas it will face competition from rival films and what begins as benign differences will escalate into justifications for enmity spanning centuries.

It's not Coca Cola v Pepsi Cola or McDonalds v Burger King – this involves MMMM – the ultimate mysteries.

The moment anything is given a permanent place on the screen, people will be willing to defend it with their lives, because, mistakenly, they will have been deceived into believing they are defending MMMM.

Branding God

In fact, all they are defending is a brand, a viewpoint, and a culturally and historically defined perspective that is as susceptible to change, as is our view of music, transport, fashion and politics.

They are dying for a whim; passing ideas that are based on nothing more substantial than a child's wide-eyed expectation that Santa Claus will come at Christmas.

There is always another film, another set of Oscars and BAFTAs and next year's offerings are even now finishing production.

We must protect the sound MMMM, from allowing anyone ever again to make their version of the sound a permanent icon and so to damn humanity to the oppression that follows.

So why the screen at all?

Why not remove MMMM from conversation and thought and discourage any screen activity? Then there would be no temptation to permanence.

It's an attractive proposition and we may evolve the wisdom and honesty to do so.

However, it's unrealistic in the short term and there may be advantages in the process.

People's religious views provide an insight into their thinking and moral basis. Their ideas about MMMM set out their conception of and their relationship with their ultimate vision.

For most, thoughts about MMMM are vested with everything that is good and so it signifies the infinite exemplar.

However, if someone claims that our relationship with MMMM must be one of awe and petition, subserviently surrendering ourselves in appreciation and obedience, flaying ourselves for our imperfections and aspiring to improve, we can protest. We can point out the negative consequences of such images and encourage them to explore others.

If another states that nothing evil can be imputed to MMMM and from this assertion deduces that when a believer claims MMMM has directed them to kill, bomb or maim others, it must be a 'good' thing to do. Then we can expose the argument's flaw and show how an unchallenged assumptive belief can lead to a devastating and errant conclusion.

The rule must be that nothing can be indelibly placed upon the screen, no assumptive beliefs and no foundational thoughts upon which to build a creedal system. The ideas flashed temporarily across the screen must always be open to the critique of others.

Esperanto of religion

Perhaps though over time, within the international arena, those screen ideas that were regarded as palatable, moral and efficacious for society as a whole could gain respectability and a utilitarian MMMM language might begin to develop.

The dream of speaking a common language has not been realised and the likelihood of arriving at an agreed language when speaking about MMMM is remote. However, it may be that the international community could identify a set of words and ideas that were universally approved as being constructive in building community and good human relations.

Perhaps MMMM could be seen as a 'divine' Secretary General of the United Nations. A world moderator, not worshipped but afforded the respect due to the position and the work involved; not in authority over, but representative of the authority borne by all; not obeyed, but seeking to elicit and facilitate the best in others.

Prayer would not be the frantic search for extra-terrestrial help but visionary and strategic thinking about how to resolve problems that beset us.

Worship would not be the mindless repetition of adulatory words to a narcissistic God, but a celebration of life.

Sacred texts would not be the Bible or other holy books but writings from any and every generation that were recognised to have merit and sagacity in enshrining and encouraging internationally agreed values and principles.

Festivals would not be centred on events in a faith's history but a calendar of celebrations and observances of common human experiences such as birth, education, relationships, families, communities, nations, suffering, ageing and death. There would also be celebrations and commemorations of historic milestones in achieving international cooperation, justice, health and peace for all.

Chapter 18

A New Way of Worshipping

Most modern worship is anachronistic with people kneeling, squatting, standing and offering repetitive stanzas to an invisible being.

Modern society is generally not able to control people for religious ends. The calls for church attendance and regular Communion go unheeded. In less developed societies, mass religious observance appears primitive and unquestioning.

If the screen is to remain empty and there is no presumptive belief that MMMM requires us to worship and every indication that it is meaningless to do so, then is there anything left *for* us to do purposefully?

Forget worship, let's originate

Alone or with others we can originate. This involves the process of beginning to explore. We start from scratch.

We may use silence, meditation or sound. We may use words, stanzas, songs or music. We may adopt different static positions or be moving. We may interact with objects such as cloth or water or foods or drinks. We may use aromas, incense, candles or flowers. We may be artistic or dance or act. We may read, teach, think of others, empathise and share hopes. We may use religious words or symbols or recognised rites. We may do anything, which is regarded as good and proper by the participants and by the international community.

Throughout the experiences, we are aware that our physicality is at play with mystery, subjectivity and art.

Explorers

We are navigating new territory, exploring new bounds. We may experience many sensations, both individually and corporately. We may make discoveries about ourselves, others and life. We may feel we have peered into the mysteries and glimpsed fresh horizons.

We may want to display all this on our screens and have others comment or, if it is innocuous, hold it close to our hearts.

However, we must keep to the discipline of keeping the screen, even our own empty.

Is there any more point to originating than there was to worshipping?

Yes, but only for those who find it creative.

No vested interests

Set rituals for worship were developed quickly and became mandatory in all the major faith traditions to give identity to the tradition, to delineate membership and require officials like priests, rabbis, and imams etc. to police the faithful. All this built a power base and had little to do with mystery.

Instead, originating is reverting to the primary creative experience that was meant to be at the heart of worship, the task of engaging with mystery.

Mystery embraced comprehensively, encompassing everything that we do not know or understand – things as basic as happiness, hope, love and optimism.

Originating does not allow anyone to exert control over our approach or our adventure, other than operating within the broadest boundaries, as set by the laws of a democratic and free society.

The originators must not be subject to artificial limitations such as precedent, tradition, habit or expectation.

Endless creativity

Originating prevents screen-filling, rejects ideas of membership, shuns fixed identity and has no need for officials. Originating is the birthright of each individual and in the gathering of individuals; is their shared treasure.

The point of originating is simple. Using every means available to mount an original expedition from the borders of our known world into the unknown mysteries beyond and within, to uncover resources for life's enhancement to achieve peace and justice for all.

It is not a licence to fantasise irresponsibly or build imaginary 'castles in the air' nor to project into the unknown and unknowable our own psychological turmoil and conundrums. Hence, there is a need to expose our inner screen activity to the fierce critique of a sceptical audience.

The legitimacy or otherwise of originating is that it must be demonstrably advantageous to the participants and to the world.

Ad hoc, anywhere, everywhere

There is no need for Cathedrals, Churches, Mosques, Temples or Synagogues, or any building designated as a holy place.

Buildings involve ownership, possession, vested interest and power, all antithetical to originating. They create a vortex greedy for finance, supporters, officials and bureaucracy. We want liberation from such entrapment.

Originating can occur in any location and is best achieved in natural surroundings or in the buildings that form part of our everyday lives and needs – our homes, community centres, pubs, clubs and hotels.

Some people have a need, emotional or circumstantial, to gather with others to originate, though the safest and best practice is alone, second with one's family and third, with one's friends.

Why alone?

There is a naked honesty about what we do in private. Stripped of everything, perhaps even our clothes. We are contained physically within the boundaries of our skin. We are unobserved.

What is the point and purpose of what we choose to do now in this solitary place?

Do we need, even here, to be noticed, to have an audience?

Do we introduce MMMM at this moment, because if not, we would do nothing, for there would be no point?

Can we strip ourselves even of our hunger, our longing and our need of MMMM and see what then happens?

Can we originate alone, truly alone?

This virginal space, where we are the sole creator and discoverer, allows our purest originating to occur. If we discover valuable resources, we must resist the temptation to rush away and evangelise others, urging them to repeat our experiments to gain similarly. By doing so, we make our experiences a commodity, like diamonds found in a mine, without realising that they may only be found in our mine, mined in our way.

This is not a selfish pursuit howe*ver*. The purpose of originating is to demonstrably improve our lives and those of others. Removing the distractions, focussing on our essential self and exploring the deep questions allow us to discern how to engage more positively with others.

Why with family?

The honesty continues. No one knows us more closely than those with whom we live or have lived, those who know our history and our ways.

Familiarity enables us to remove every pretension and reach both the nadir and zenith of another.

Originating with our loved ones sifts away delusions and pretences and leaves a residue that must have meaning or the practice is quickly shunned.

It must never be coerced or required. There is no room for dictatorial parents demanding that their children be involved or domineering spouses bringing pressure upon their partners.

Originating must be fun and have a clear benefit. It should not be ritualised or practiced monotonously but with imagination and alacrity.

Why with friends?

Again, the vein of honesty is key. Every person has a natural community of those with whom they associate and those with whom they choose to spend their time recreationally. These comprise a mix of past acquaintances, work colleagues, hobby and sport mates, neighbours etc.

When a special event is planned they provide the basis for invites.

The characters involved and their alliances are understood.

This personal community shares a history and new circumstances and choices are judged against this background.

The intrinsic danger of Church

Church is an artificial community based upon vested interest.

Politics, back biting, intrigue, cliques and affairs abound, as strangers are required to associate under the control of religion and its priestly officers.

There are no inviolable long-term loyalties or relationship commitments. Every member remains expendable and belongs only so long as they remain compliant and useful.

One damning illustration of this is how many elderly, infirm and housebound people there are whom their local church never visits, although they used to be regular church attendees.

While they filled the pews, sang the hymns and put money in the collection they were church 'family'. When they became incontinent and were languishing at home they lost the privilege of 'family' membership and were abandoned.

The beauty of home

One's home is the perfect place to originate naturally.

The relationships within the home express the quality of love.

The experiences of sharing food together and with invited guests express the quality of communion.

The special events, birthdays, anniversaries and festivals express the quality of celebration.

Gratitude for being housed securely, joy at being warm and clean, appreciation for food and family life, generosity towards friends and strangers, compassion for those in different circumstances are all marks of natural originating which need no artificial rituals.

A family may choose to share moments of reflection before eating or to sing a song together.

They may light candles at the meal table or sit in the garden looking at the stars.

They may hold hands listening to a symphony (or a rap).

They may devise ways in which they can experiment with a variety of aesthetic and sensual experiences to intensify their saturation of life and its possibilities.

However, these are some of the more formal ways of originating. The most potent remain the natural ebb and flow of positive and respectful living.

Chapter 19

The Noisy Spiritual Journey from Faith through Agnosticism and Atheism to Silence

Most evangelists and religious leaders establish strategies to lead people from a lack of belief to the point of conversion. They speak of a spiritual journey from the darkness to the light and the need to consolidate one's faith as a person matures as a disciple.

They perceive the journey's end to be full committed membership to Christ expressed by regular involvement in the life of the church.

This route perversely often entraps people and leads them away from the truth in which they could have found their liberation.

Everyone has faith. They choose to place their trust and confidence in many things and people. They have faith that the sun will rise and water will come from their tap; that their partner loves them and their friends respect them.

The way they live their lives is the present expression of all they have experienced up until the present.

Their thoughts and choices are rooted in their lives and circumstances.

When asked about 'God' they have few answers and many vague ideas.

If a salesman or woman manages to sell them the Christian package, they begin to believe there is a treasure chest of knowledge to acquire that will provide them with all that is known about God.

Trickery

Trading standards should really be able to intervene. The unsuspecting convert enters a labyrinth out of which they may never emerge. However, if they have the wherewithal to keep questioning and challenging what they are told, or life's experiences reveal the lies that are surrounding them they will realise at some juncture that the chest has little treasure and is nothing to do with God.

Spurred on, they may examine all the other 'treasure chests' of faith held by every religion that exists. This may be a rapid process, but often a person meanders tortuously through the obstacles of various faith products.

The journey will bring them to a moment of intense enlightenment that no such God, as humanity has described, could exist. They are confident that every religious word, dogma and practice is thoroughly human. Religion's tower of Babel has suddenly come crashing down around them. They place their faith in atheism.

Truth

Truth continues to press them forward. Atheism feels too rigid. A watertight system as neatly conceived as Christianity, decrying deities as firmly as religionists affirm them. They find themselves washed up on the shores of agnosticism. It seems that their destination, at the end of such a monumental journey, has to be specific and definable, even if in the negative.

The human quest is to construct, materially, verbally and philosophically.

Agnosticism provides a respectable citadel within which to house all the knowledge gained.

However, it's a phantasm.

The only true destination available for us to reach is to stand in the presence of mystery, of all that is not known and to be silent. No fracturing of the airwaves with meaningless grunts or packing the mind with retro items. The silence respects our limitations and our lack of knowledge.

In the silence we encounter awe, intrigue, curiosity, speculation, fear, apprehension, terror, hope; in fact a spectrum of reactions which energise and motivate us.

In that electrifying place at the threshold of the unknown we can rue the choice that we once made to turn away from this new world to the inferior realm of platitude.

Now we can see clearly though the charlatans who peddled certainty and the dogmatic corporations advertising 'truths'.

Here notions of gods, rulers, omnipotents, sacred books and divine texts appear as playthings from the nursery.

Determination

The silence begets determination.

The mystery teases us.

It excites our desire and fires our passion.

We become incensed at all that has held us back, diverted us and made us quiescent.

We become again explorers, adventurers and pioneers, foraging ahead.

Defiantly we rip the apple from the tree and sink our teeth into its delicious and informative juice.

We refuse to allow the multiplicity of languages to impede our desire to storm the walls of heaven.

We force an entrance before the human Gods of earth's imaginings and topple them from their artificial thrones.

We put in place human governance and invite the public to range free over heaven's realms.

The journey continues

Traditionally, the religious believer feels they have discovered the true faith and can relax. They even promote the assertion that their God 'never changes'.

Reality shows otherwise. Change is constant. Creation and destruction are continual cycles. Unless we engage energetically with all that surrounds us we signal the surrender to our decline.

While ever we have breath, our minds should seek knowledge

and our bodies should seek exercise. We should question everything and base our lives and our thinking on what is known.

Our speculations, hunches and hypotheses may form part of the process of exploration, but we must never claim they represent fact, only a conceptual framework to try and plumb further depths.

If evidence exposes them to be flawed, even prejudicial to our development, they should quickly and humbly be discarded.

Ironically, the believer clinging to the life raft of a fixed God in a world of change overlooks that God is in as constant a state of flux, remodelled and newly conceived by each generation. Altered states are unavoidable.

A religion-free world

So the resolute must press ahead despite this cloying conservatism.

We must confront humanity's apparent reticence to accept the premise that we are responsible for ourselves.

Let's imagine if all religious thinking were jettisoned.

Imagine if our experience upon the earth was regarded as finite and final?

If it were just you, your life and this world.

I would suggest that this is the place of truth at which all brave truth seekers will in the end meet.

This is the place from which we can truly begin to live our lives.

This is the point that we can bring honour and find unity over our pre-occupation with MMMM, when we accept finally the mantle of responsibility for everything that is ours.

If I put this is in clear traditional language.

It is only when we stop believing in God and stop thinking about God and stop praying to God and stop worshipping God and stop having anything to do with God or giving any thought to God that we can be true.

Then alone can it be assessed whether we are thinking and living, as we ought?

Is this the ultimate blasphemy?

Believers across the world may be incensed at such a suggestion. My son, on hearing the content of the book worried:

'Won't someone firebomb our home Dad? Will your life not be in danger?'

It appears to take so little to provide fanatics with an excuse for radical protest and even mild-mannered religionists to take to the streets. At times such reactions and the threats that accompany them turn sinister and life-threatening. Bounty has even been promised to those who murder a critic perceived to be a blasphemer.

I would contend though that there is absolutely no blasphemy in this book.

I hope what is apparent is my disenchantment with every system of belief emanating from humanity. The descriptions given by human beings about God are flawed and inaccurate.

We need to jettison all the language we use about God and all the beliefs and rituals we have about God because they are human inventions masquerading as truth and fact. They are impostors, confusing and deceiving humanity.

However, there is NO blasphemy involved, for this simple reason.

'God' (MMMM) will be delighted (if 'God' (MMMM) is found to exist), that we have finally realised our arrogance and folly in claiming things we did not know and will laud our courage in ridding ourselves of our religious humbug.

We have journeyed into a place of truth

The place where we realise we have nothing of merit on the subject to say.

The place that leads us to silence.

No bad thing.

No blasphemy.

Chapter 20

It's That Old Devil Called God Again

If the truth is that we know nothing about 'God', should stop being obsessed with 'God' and must resign 'God' to history, why is it that 'God' has been such an enduring factor in the human psyche?

In the multifarious journey of our evolution, why has the physical world led us to delude ourselves into worshipping divinities?

Why have we not only chased a dream but also squandered so much in appeasing our religious need?

Surely, as a pointless and counterproductive part of our development, God's influence over us would have gradually receded until only a vestige remained.

Some may argue that this process is underway in the more educated and advanced societies and minds, however, it still meets fierce resistance even in these quarters.

Method in the madness

Academics have traced the increasing complexity of human society and the attributes upon which our enmeshment relies. The emergence of morality and social esteem has been identified as an equally curious feature as religion. Why would a *spe*cies, acquiring cognitive awareness, begin to establish ethical codes and become sensitive to public censure?

Studies have concluded that acceptable behaviour grew to become a vital requirement to gain inclusion within a group. Such membership was essential because the group had the power to defend itself, forage for food and harbour its offspring, whereas exclusion meant almost certain death.

As awareness grew, so did the observation of human behaviour and the expectation that certain social mores would be followed. The simple behavioural patterns that once had provided cohesion to the species became increasingly complex.

It was necessary to introduce mechanisms to bolster conformity and strengthen the sense of accountability.

Conscience

This individual monitoring faculty upon which we all rely to a greater or lesser extent enables us to assess our choices and decide upon courses of actions. It spawns an internal conversation between good and bad, expedient and honest, advantageous and damaging, right and wrong, socially palatable or taboo. It acts as our internal light and moral compass, by which we chart our direction.

Bolstering this faculty are the means by which others have the opportunity to spy on our lives, naturally or artificially. Those who share our homes, our streets, and our places of work as well as our methods of transit provide the eyes that help keep us in check and true to society's customs. In our modern age, CCTV and other methods of electronic surveillance reinforce our sometimes weak espousal of social etiquette.

But all of these are insufficient, as the burgeoning prison population indicates.

Ultimately, people choose what they do in the privacy of their own minds and carry out those choices in secret. Their ability to relativise their choices and to find moral permission for them is a subjective and flawed process prone to error and self-delusion and can often lead to catastrophe. It seems we are adept at developing a myopic vision that sees the world from a blinkered and distorted perspective.

Enter God

God is the ultimate CCTV provision. As the Anglican Mass

prayer states, 'Almighty God, to whom all hearts are open, all desires known and from whom no secrets are hidden'.

This is 24/7 comprehensive inescapable surveillance.

Attach this to laws and commandments and mix this with dire warnings of hellfire for deviancy and you evolve a pretty fail-safe policing system. Maximise the take up of the evolutionary appendage by talking up its benefits – heaven, a benevolent creator, a miracle provider, a guardian angel etc.

Ensure that the 'God' figure is made in the image of the species concerned and is continuingly malleable, reflecting advances in their understanding, and you have a potent weapon against disorder and a resource to promote good. Its drawback is that it is proving to have a limited shelf life.

Such a mechanism, based on deceit and lacking an objective base is, at some point, going to be exposed. If not by knowledge alone then by the empirical realisation that God's policing role is increasingly ineffective in a modern analytical society.

Swathes of devotees pack into St Peter's Square to adulate the Pope and declare allegiance to Catholicism. However, their lives concede choices that prove they have jettisoned any fear that God is watching them. They do what they like, irrespective of church or divine teaching. They practice contraception, have sex outside of marriage, undergo IVF and opt for abortions, yet they retain their dependence on and expectation of God's bountiful provision.

It is clear that they are psychologically dependent on a 'God factor' in their lives but one designed and manufactured in the workshop of their brain, with no independent existence. They cling irrationally to their deistic approach as a cocaine addict does to their supply.

Others, finding the divine police station raided and now empty descend into anarchic behaviour, released from their divine tag, believing that the world is for their pleasure and not their responsibility.

Evolving beyond the need for God

If religion was a naturally produced concept to resource and safeguard a particular stage in our development, then the question posed is what should replace it?

A reductionist assessment of the God mechanism identifies that its benefit to a person is the awareness that they are being observed.

All of us can relate to this easily.

We are aware that we feel quite different if people are watching us than when we are alone. This difference varies according to what we are doing. In the event of considering a course of action that is of a dubious moral value, the attention of others can have a marked effect.

Being observed, particularly by those who can ensure we suffer the appropriate consequences for our actions, can prevent the mildest to the most severe breach of society's protocols.

The 'Big Brother' State

Human observation though may be insufficient. At times people will act up to attention and be deliberately offensive or destructive in front of a crowd, believing they will get away with it.

The advances we have made scientifically and electronically in being able to capture, record, retrieve, identify and store evidence are essential aspects of making the 'God' factor redundant.

If CCTV, audio recordings, images and DNA can accompany witness statements then the culpable have nowhere to hide. The world can watch their behaviour or be informed about it, assess it and pass judgement.

Internalising

As we learn to take greater responsibility for our lives and take back the powers and functions devolved to God, there is an urgency to perfect our own internal monitoring system.

It is based on a simple tenet – if the whole world were watching me now what would they think?

This may seem like a further devolution of power, rather it is exposing individual thought to communal scrutiny. Can I present a cogent defence of my thoughts to the world and will my arguments find favour?

If not, am I able to justify my choices to myself and do I have the moral conviction, based upon reason, that my intentions are honourable, and if misunderstood in the present, will gain respect in the future.

The loss of God

It is not only God's moderating and policing role that must be replaced but also the pervading sense of resource and assistance. The mythology that there is a munificent grain store in the sky must translate itself into self-sufficiency and reliance upon an inter-dependent and co-operative world in which we have an integral part to play in ensuring the common good.

The benefits of removing God from the picture

People may be too afraid of going it alone, as though we were bound to become unstuck and face a ruinous future. We began though by surveying our calamitous past and present. In taking greater responsibility for our actions, in society expanding the network of surveillance and in the world enshrining codes of conduct in international law, a more optimistic prospect beckons.

Chapter 21

Why It's So Hard to Let Go of God

Sometimes I have the most wonderful dreams that I can fly. They are vivid and I wake thrilled and satisfied. It's a skill in my dream that seems an integral part of my physicality. I stretch out my arms and find myself ascending. I soar high; brush the tops of the trees, dive and swoop. It is the most exhilarating experience.

I like to interpret dreams and find they are most i*ll*uminating, so often relevant to my current life or situation. The flying dreams intrigued me. From where did they come and what did they represent? How could it be that I appeared experientially to understand what the sensation of flying like a bird would be like?

Recently, I was riveted while walking in a park. I saw something I had seen so many times before, but this time it provided a missing link that connected a series of ragged thoughts.

A father had lifted his baby high above his head. He held her by the stomach so that she was in a flight position and walked with her lifting her up and down and side to side.

I could suddenly superimpose myself as the baby and imagine my own father scooping me high. Of course I have no actual conscious memories of this happening. If it happened, it is laid deep in those mysterious years beyond the reach of our conscious memories.

Those all-important early years

Every parent remains mystified that their children have hardly any memories of all the special times they shared with them as babies and toddlers in the pre-school years.

How could it be possible that holidays and Christmas times and Adventure playgrounds and presents and the laughter and excitement of those years could have left no lasting impression?

In fact the impression is so lasting as to be life-changing and possibly inerasable.

The newborn is helpless and entirely dependent. At best, milk, liquids, foods, warmth, cuddles and comfort are provided. The *b*aby's needs are satisfied routinely as if by right by resources beyond itself and over which she or he has little control. In time and particularly if there is a failure to care, techniques to influence the provision and exert control over the provider emerge, such as crying and screaming.

At worst, the baby may find herself/himself given little of anything and struggles on the edge of survival. Wherever they find themselves on the relative scale of abundance to dearth affects them profoundly and predisposes them in nature beyond their control or understanding.

An adult may wake with an implicit sense that all is well with the world, whereas another may rise feeling unloved and as though the world is against them. Neither can pinpoint from where that foundational feeling comes. As though there was a hidden control room deep within them into which they cannot gain access.

The impressionable years

Then comes those early years from which we can retrieve snatches of hazy memory. Odd cameos of sensation and experience, often muddled and inaccurate but which point to the emergence of a memory capability seared with significant moments.

Again, these are years replete with intense events of which we have only a minimal sense. However, it is clear that within the infinite possibilities of a child's upbringing, there is one common overarching theme.

The place of their predominant carers is critical; whether mother, father, extended family members or other third parties, the individual/s concerned become the identified lead figure/s in the child's world. They provide, guide, discipline and rule.

The child becomes a subject in their dominion

This model of the child's earliest engagement with their life is formative of their perceptions, approaches and beliefs and their living patterns into and through adulthood.

Integral to the model are the following attributes:

A hierarchy of authority – the parent/carer rules and the child is ruled.

An arbitrary system of distributing resources – based on the subjective approach of the parent/carer.

A relationship of subservience – in which the child has to function efficiently to maximise her or his benefit.

The ritualised pattern of expected behaviour – that involves asking, receiving, thanking, behaving and apologising in an expected manner.

The satisfaction of the parent/carer – to ensure that the child's world is as sweet as possible.

The sense that their whole world derives from their parent/carer – their life, provisions, rules, happiness, safety, freedom, protection.

The transition from singular parental or carer rule to a co-operative institutional rule managed by the parents/carers, school and society.

The sharing of hierarchical power with the institutions' heads (Health Visitor, Head Teacher, Social Worker, Chief Constable, Prime Minister etc.).

The same patterns of subjective resource distribution – Tower block living or exclusive suburbia, Grammar, Secondary, Comprehensive or private schools, private or public health etc.

The requirement of subservient living, ritualised patterns of expected behaviour and the need to satisfy the 'establishment' for one's safety.

The sense that a person's whole world derives from and

depends upon living within prescribed boundaries.

Programmed, conditioned and robotic adults

When we consider the deeply engrained conditioning of a child to perceive the world in this manner it is of little surprise that launched as an independent adult they feel bereft, frightened and in acute need of replacing their lost world with imitative structures.

Their bedrock knowledge emanates from a mysteri*ou*s and unidentifiable primary source of life and supply; at best, an ever present provider and protector to whom they could appeal for help and succour and be in receipt of a response that brought relief and resolution.

Then faces were given to this provision in the form of parent/carer/head/institution, but all of them were transitory. In addition, however good they were, they were never perfect, and the evolutionary drive is to source the optimal supply and the perfect environment.

The combination of this insatiable thirst for perfection and the mysterious encounter with the anonymous provision of early infancy provides the blueprint for navigating the adult world.

It produces largely compliant citizens contributing to our hierarchical institutionalised society as well as underpinning our vital quest to discover or reinstate a paradisiacal state.

As paradise eludes us on earth, we are susceptible to the belief that it exists nevertheless elsewhere and while earthly parents/carers and rulers of every kind may have failed, we jump to the belief that they are mere shadows of the ultimate source of life, authority and provision to whom we can appeal, the God of all.

Mummy… Daddy

It's a humbling observation that the great religionists, theologians, professors and devout academics of past and present were actually only really continuing to say, "Mummy" or "Daddy".

When we consider the time, money, resources and lives that have been squandered in the vacuous pursuit of that imaginary infant idyll we are forced to pause and reflect.

The enormity of the self-deceit, evolution's trick and the insanity of our emergent species quietens us finally.

Can we really grow up and leave home?

Perhaps a lump comes to our throats. We characterised ourselves as so mature, confident and balanced. Now we begin to realise we have spent so long and wasted so much, attached to the proverbial 'apron strings' of our childhood.

All those church services, prayers, religious discussions, scriptural readings, missions, outreaches, fundraising events for church bells, roofs, hymn books and refurbishments. They were all the vain thrashings of the child within desperate to replace their lost mother and father.

A door appears finally before us.

Are we bold enough to truly wave goodbye and set out alone?

Sufficiency

The critical anxiety that assails us is whether we have the wherewithal to manage on our own?

Will we survive if we have to believe in ourselves and internalise all we have learnt. Can we cope if we have to be our own provider, protector, guide and rescuer? Have we acquired the necessary self-confidence and maturity to venture out into the big wide world as responsible adults?

Such a challenge does not mean we are islands, disconnected from others; much more respectful contributors to a community based on realities and not fantasies. Amidst the plethora of activities and challenges, one volatile and contaminating ingredient will not feature. There will be no talk about or recourse to Gods or religion.

Great respect will be afforded to that which is known and a humble silence over that which is not.

The adults will know they must make their own decisions, provide for their own needs, arrive at their own conclusions, appeal to their own better natures and set for themselves their own rules, for all of which they will remain responsible and accountable.

Crisis

When we are facing our greatest challenges and feel forlorn and abandoned, we will be aware of the infant response mechanism kicking in deep within our psyches, urging us to call out in prayer to that 'mysterious provider' that came out of the mists when we were babies and met our needs.

Instead, we will replace the hazy image with the focused knowledge that there was no mystery then or now. A parent came to give us milk or change our nappy. Now we are the adults who must work out our own path through the maelstrom. Now we must source the milk and clear up our mess for it is no one else's task and certainly not 'God's!

Religion as cradle

Some may protest that attending a holy place, saying prayers or offering worship are innocuous pastimes that cause no harm and should not be criticised. If they bring comfort then all well and good.

I suggest the opposite. There is clearly a problem if a group of adults begin to suck dummies or climb into cradles or revert to wearing nappies. Regressive behaviour should not be encouraged and needs to be reversed. A healthy trajectory is away from childhood dependencies and fairy tale comforts into independent living and thinking.

Religion presents a counter force, herding us into infantile rhythms, finding advantage in disabling our maturation and feeding off our insecurities.

There is no ombudsperson or watchdog to highlight abuses and no professional body to maintain standards. A religion can claim anything about their 'invisible' God and the requirements its adherents must follow. Even when others can point out inconsistencies, illogicalities, immoralities and the plain nonsense in a religion's belief system and its claims about God, all are as water from a duck's back for the believer.

They remain as incapable of responding cogently as a baby does to criticism of their parent.

Kind God versus cruel God

Our psychological programming is established very early with all the pervading models supplied from childhood. There is a vital link between what happened to us as babies and infants and how we view the world and what we believe.

If a child is raised in a male dominated home where the father is the authority figure and the mother remains submissive, then the espousal of a male deity and hierarchical authority might well follow.

If a child experiences their mother and father sharing authority and decision making on an equitable basis, then a God beyond a singular gender and individual control could be more appealing.

If a child experiences a home where communal decisions are made, in which each member of the family however young or old is given the chance to contribute and affect the life of the family, then a divinity or good energy, diffuse and common to all would feel most appropriate.

If a child is at the receiving end of a disciplinarian meting out corporal punishment, then it may well be that their God is no stranger to rules and violent sanctions.

If a child knows favouritism and advantage then the idea that their God might select them as a chosen one for a promised land could follow.

If a child knows blight, want and abuse, it may well be that a vengeful God fits the bill to bring retribution upon her or his tormentors and rescue the child/adult to a heaven beyond this world.

There are many possibilities. Once the link has been made between our childhood and our later beliefs and choices, we may well be intrigued to explore, as much as may still be in reach, exactly what did happen to us as babies and early infants, before memory gives us a reliable evidence trail.

Re-appraisal

Relatives, records, social history, photographs, newspapers etc. all may shed light on the world into which we were born and the prevailing attitudes within which we were raised.

We can bring to bear our adult perceptions and analysis to the character of our father and mother and to the quality of their relationship and the shenanigans of their lives. We can project back what it would have been like to be raised by them. What position we held within the family. How we related to any siblings. Once we have gathered as much evidence as possible about our backgrounds we can face the ultimate question.

In what sort of God did all of this predispose us to believe?

The flip side

As we begin to make sense of the subjective, random *and* very unreliable manner by which we construct our fundamental belief systems and experiment with detaching ourselves from our reliance upon them, a tantalising new world beckons.

A world in which we can, as liberated adults, make sense of that which we know and choose a path more readily our own, in which fantasies and divine projections are removed and we can walk tall and confident in the here and now, leaving the unknown to the time of its discovery.

Chapter 22

A More Sinister Reckoning

There is another more urgent impetus to rid ourselves of God-talk and another reason why it's so hard to jettison.

When we examine some of our basic beliefs about God and recognise that they represent our human projections and we realise that in truth we are examining what lies within us, much of what we find is problematic. It forms a convoluted mix of good and bad blended into a hotchpotch of fantasy.

The impossibility of religion becomes clearer

Our beliefs give us a 'God' that is thoroughly infected from the outset, because she/he/it comes from infected goods. God is humanity writ large; a divine being that is a caricature model of our best and worst, a mad mannequin that haunts us with promises and with perils.

The perfect 'me'

So let's unpack what we really want, deep beneath, in those hidden illusive depths of our minds.

We want to be powerful. We imagine ourselves to be the ruler of our world, dispensing favour and fury at choice and whim. We imagine the hordes worshipping us and paying homage to us. We are stimulated by the potency of our position and produce images of the miracles and wonders we could perform and the awe occasioned in our subjects.

Our resources are limitless. Vast in wisdom, we are able to solve the impossible and confound the strategies of others. Nothing is beyond our capabilities.

These are the foolhardy pretensions of youth and the delusions of the insane. In the real world, we are all too well aware of our limitations but they become satisfactorily attractive to us when packaged respectably in a God.

Worship me

Oh to be worshipped and adored. Imagine if the world chose to bow at our feet. Wherever we went, fans would fawn over us, adore us, ask for our autographs and desire us. We would command such respect and such adulation. Everyone would want to be in our company, to laugh at our jokes and benefit from our friendship. Our Facebook page and Twitter stream would be bursting with billions of friends and followers.

Our every word and every move would be followed and scrutinised. A twitch, a frown and gesture would all be latched upon for meaning and purpose. Groupies would camp outside our every location and 24/7 coverage of our lives would be beamed around the world.

Fame, celebrity would hold nothing in comparison to this unprecedented intensity of eternal worship.

Deep down it seems, we play around with such delusions of grandeur. We don't like to admit such things to ourselves. We act coy, shy and modest. We allow ourselves our five minutes of fame. However, most of the time, unless we are particularly exhibitionist or extrovert, we settle for a conventional diet of family and friends giving us appropriate attention and due respect and affection.

In place of our lost dreams we vaunt a God onto whom we foist all these destructive and subliminal drives. God receives, on our behalf, what should really have been ours and as we join the train of devotees, we are actually paying homage to ourselves.

Superhero sadist

We can see ourselves apparently leaping to intervene in crisis situations, producing the ultimate solution to intractable problems, providing the way out of tricks and traps and being the constant on-call emergency service. We want to be the answer to every problem and to astonish the world with our resource and ability.

Our heart is the biggest ever, pumping with love for a broken world, reaching out to the forlorn and downtrodden, there to feed the hungry, heal the sick and release the unjustly imprisoned.

We are judge and jury, the dispenser of justice and the arbiter of right and wrong. Our word is law and our choices righteous.

The dark side rules too, for our base desires must gain vent. As ultimate ruler we have the power to take away life as well as to give it, to punish as well as to bless, to choose when and if to help. What might seem wicked and immoral if done by a Satan, is accommodated and renamed if done by a God. So the world lies before us to torment, ravage and destroy at our whim.

We wield the power to create and to crush and in our realistic assessment of our own limited arts we devolve such extreme cruelty and kindness to our puppet God. Meanwhile we practice a more modest version among those around us.

Choose me

That terrible playground sinking feeling when the captains are not picking you and slowly you are being left until you reach that unenviable position of being last and you have to walk towards the team that grudgingly has to have you.

We want to be the first in the queue, the one specially selected, the name called out above all others, the winner of the raffle, the winning ticket holder on the lottery, the favoured one and the spoilt one.

We want special arrangements to have been made for us, preferential treatment among others, titles, deference, obsequious acknowledgements of our power, position and status.

The brutal truth is that we are just ants, grains of sand and as common as the grass of the fields. It is too great an insult to the raging protesting monster inside us.

Don't people realise who we are, what we are and how we should be treated?

If not by the rabble around us, then these needs will be fulfilled by our God protégé. The divine one will choose us above all others, predestine us as her/his son or her/his daughter, especially commission us for a unique task upon the earth as part of a unique main plan underway. This God will call us out first, choose us for the eternal team, and provide us with pride of place.

It appears to matter little that billions of others believe the same, meaning there are a lot of other 'chosen' ones. We choose not to cloud our smug satisfaction with such awkward comparisons. What makes us warm inside is that we are chosen.

We are not troubled that our warmth necessitates another's cold and that when we skip over to the Divine team; we leave others languishing at the wall. In fact the sadistic side of us delights in their misfortune. Anyway, it's all just and proper, because God has done it.

Cut the poverty lark, where's my real estate?

It seems we all want only the best. Our just deserts are a billionaire mansion in folding acres of green, with crystal lakes, velvet forests, breathtaking views and every gadget available. We want family and friends available to party and enemies not only deleted but also tormented in some hellish slum shantytown existence.

We believe it's only right that we should be the richest and the most benefited individuals. The fact that we may be grubbing about struggling to find food or pay a heating bill or satisfy a debt company is all a huge mistake. So our true reward is just around the corner, when the trumpets will sound and the limo will sweep us into our heaven.

True, we will pass the unfortunates at the gate, covered in

sores. Somehow, it comforts us. It reminds us from where we have come and what we have achieved and why we are different from others. Why we reside properly in this paradise and others are consigned to hell.

Suffering – our trump card

As our inner monster marauds and we justify our inner muddled world, we ensure we are immune from criticism. When others cast caustic remarks our way about our inexperience and our unwillingness to engage and our lack of trauma, we ridicule the shallowness of their remarks. Don't they realise how much we have suffered. We have taken the world upon our shoulders.

We have died an infinite number of deaths, sucked the sin from the world, been hung out to dry. Their mockery has nailed us high.

We are members of that elite group of honourable people willing to sacrifice their lives for others. Of course they can't see that or know that, so our God demonstrates it for them, our suffering, crucified, dying God.

Further, when under attack, if anyone begins to delude themselves that we are their plaything, a victim for their excesses, then let them witness the power within us to transform our enemy's worst onslaught into an escape route to true freedom. Resurrection. We are untouchable and invincible for we have the keys beyond this fleeting shadow world.

Discrimination

However politically correct we may be, there is this greedy beast at play demanding advantage and second *h*elpings, pushing their way to the front of any queue and expecting truffles and champagne.

Our hotline to the interventionist God is the epitome of this prejudice. You're not healing everyone, but do heal me. You are not choosing to feed these starving children but I expect my dinner tonight. You overlook these languishing prisoners, hostages, refugees and drowning boat people but attend to this parking ticket, this need for me not to be late, for my child to pass the test, to any amount of trivia that I may pass your way, O divine answer to my indulged expectation.

Our God has no qualms about acting with ruthless self-interest to meet our daily requirements.

That is why we think nothing of pushing ourselves forward, why we can cope with TV images of the starving and desperate, why we are immune to burning Syrian children and decapitated prisoners.

Our God wouldn't allow such a thing to happen to us.

It's all right dear daughter/precious son – it's all forgiven

It's shocking how easily we let ourselves off the hook. We read reports about the court testimony of the convicted and are chilled at the ability of those found guilty of war crimes, genocide, murder, rape, torture or any of the gross inhumanities we inflict on each other to pardon their actions.

They nearly always have a denial, a justification or a watered down version of their crimes. They can quite readily live with themselves despite what they have done.

We apply the same discretion to all of our misdemeanours, great or small.

We have a self-protecting facility to forgive our capacity to commit evil. What others find incomprehensible appears quite plain to us as we attempt to explain.

The incredulity of others and their meanness in offering forgiveness is overcome by a munificent God, who embraces us with open arms, however prodigal we have been, clothes us with the finest attire and fare and restores us to our former glory.

The past wiped clean, the future bright; there is nothing that jams the ever-rolling stream of this antidote to our heinous or selfish actions.

I'm delicious

The final aberration is when our self-love becomes so extreme that we declare that we are delectable.

We see ourselves as so sought after that we should be eaten as the finest this world can offer. We are the elixir of life, the panacea of all that is ill, and the prophylactic against all disease. Consume us by being with us, listening to us, ingesting us in some form just once a day or once a week or once a month and all will be well, your life improved.

We externalise this by claiming that our God is so prized he too is a consumable. However the base impulses within us ensure that we must have precedence. So we set ourselves up over our ultimate icon. Though she/he is God, God ends up on our plate, in our stomachs and finally in the sewer. We are supreme and so we dine at the head of the table and eat the God of the world.

Too hot to handle

An essential part of our maturing is mapping out our inner world and working to tame, control and direct all we discover there. If you have found this chapter upsetting, I urge you not to despair about what lurks beneath.

You may protest that you don't recognise any of the above. However, I suggest most of it lurks in that subconscious world beyond our grasp. We can though identify its presence in many of our actions and thinking.

I intend this book to be positive and enlightening. If we can face these challenges we can evolve into stronger more integrated human beings.

The chaotic and disturbing forces we have uncovered within are the primitive components of our evolutionary history. As we have striven for predominance as a species and as individuals, believing in the following has been important:

That we are worthy of worship, omnipotent and omniscient;

That we are superheroes and so attract positions of advantage;

That we are willing to be cruel to instil fear and protect our position;

That we have the power to dispense or withhold favour;

That we deserve the best;

That we are invincible, even stronger than death;

That we can act as we choose to gain our best;

That we can tolerate any personal behaviour, however foul;

That we have the right to consume and control;

That we can create a deity to make all the above legitimate.

These are basic animal instincts from which we have sculpted a monstrous God. It is time to evolve further.

A more balanced view

We are well aware that the undue attention involved in celebrity corrupts those adored and those adoring. We know that superheroes do not exist other than for the occasional random acts of those who have managed to be brave when required. We realise that favouritism is damaging to all involved. We are resigned to the truth that while we can grow through suffering, it remains a scourge to be eradicated. We rage at death. We detest discrimination. We must ensure amends have been made and true change achieved before offering forgiveness to others or ourselves. We ought to consume less and more respectfully, stop devouring the planet and other people's share of it; prevent other people consuming us and guard against the practice of ever consuming others and that includes deities!

The path to civilisation involves the taming of the human beast within us. When that is achieved, the need for a divine beast is removed.

Chapter 23

But You are an Archbishop and Wear a Cross

You Say Prayers and Take Services.

How Can You Write Such a Book?

Am I a hypocrite, or have I managed to escape the trickery, deceit and shackles of a traditional approach to and understanding of religion?

The Gardens of Paradise

Perhaps, if you have been brave enough to read this book and have arrived here with me, you may be ready to take my hand as we part the trailing ivy and enter the gardens of paradise.

It may seem that a long time has passed since the start of the book, when you began to break out from the entrapment of others and started this journey of discovery.

However, this sacred vale is the fruit of your courage and endeavour.

At peace with yourself

The expectations of parents, friends and family have been laid aside.

The teachings and snares of others have been recognised.

The dictates of every human God have been relinquished.

In this inner garden there is just you, alone, totally alone… happily alone… contentedly alone… at peace.

In this garden you can see and deeply appreciate goodness, justice and truth.

You choose to be good and just and true, because it is evidently the most moral, fulfilling and life-enhancing approach to life.

At peace with others

From your vantage point, you can see all the land arrayed before you, upon which every other person lives and moves, with all their differences, and you know that they began their earthly sojourn just as you. You have a profound love for them all.

You understand the unity of humanity and the common bonds that bind us inextricably together.

You are aware of the depths of evil and the moral heights of which all are capable.

You cherish all people, including yourself, and grieve for their heartache, agonise over their suffering, rue their mistakes and urge their success.

Every mother, father, sibling, relative, spouse, child is as your own.

You come alongside all people, respecting their language, culture, faith and experience. You can see them, fresh born, pools of innocence and know their days and walk in their shoes and understand.

No one is your enemy, not even the one that takes your life or burns your home, because you perceive the enemy is within you as much as without. This is not meant as an airy-fairy platitude but a robust declaration that we are all implicated in evil acts; pointing a finger is not an option, nor bombing and destroying an externally identified enemy. Drones, cluster bombs, land mines and invasions are out.

So you pledge yourself to work the ground, to create and tend to the world, that it might become an outer garden, mirroring the paradise you are cultivating within you from which all can benefit.

You enter the struggle to overcome poverty, end injustice, rid the world of the gross disparities of wealth and privilege and establish the means by which all can enjoy an equitable experience of life.

At peace with the world

You are in awe at the teeming, burgeoning **ear**th and its effulgent sun. The majesty of the natural world defies description. Intricacy and artwork beyond imagination absorb your wonder and elicit your worship.

In the orbs of morning dew that garland rose petals and spiders' webs, your eye casts across the expanse of all that exists and knows the ecstasy of a willing and positive surrender to the cycle of life.

At peace with MMMM

No more anguished searching and fretful debate. The life-draining and denying discipleships are over.

It is yours to do and to do well if you can and others may have to pick up the pieces if you can't.

Peering into the unknown is like lying on the soft grass and losing yourself in the vaults of sky and cloud, liberated into the immensity of blues and whites. There are no answers.

The birds soar, the trees sway, a dog barks and on a far hill a cow roams.

It is yours also to be, and not to know all things.

Your unassailable confidence is that whoever/whatever MMMM points towards and/or wants you to be, you can stop wasting time musing and speculating and get on with the job of being your best.

At peace with the insanities

Bullets, bombs, devastation, abuse, war, hunger, disease, corruption, tyranny, torture, inequalities, injustice, political oppression, genocide…

Walls and boundaries, prisons and exclusions, possessions and power games…

Intimidation, bullying, isolation and prejudice…

Cocktails of evil served up with terror to torment…

But none that are potent enough to remove the peace of this garden.

Here is an inviolable place, an inner oasis that is the wellspring and infinite resource for life.

Nothing can dislodge the mental strength and the spiritual maturity that arises from its discovery.

It equips a person to be a world citizen and an ambassador for all that is good.

Its benefits are open to anyone and are not dependent on any one philosophical system. The poorest and most uneducated people can find their way here, though they are vulnerable to those peddling promises of paradise beyond.

Surprisingly, it's hard for those with economic advantage to arrive. Their paths are blocked by countless predatory influences and most die while taking a circuitous diversion into affluence and religion.

At peace with one's own insanities

As flawed human beings though, don't we continue to bring insanity into this garden of paradise ourselves?

Yes.

That explains why there is a lake of crystal waters at its heart, in which we can bathe.

These are the waters of truth. Looking upon their surface we can see ourselves as we are and as others see us. Slipping under their flow we can be washed clean of the past and find healing in the present and assuage our thirst for the future. We can emerge refreshed and replenished with our hearts set to make amends and to strive to do better.

Archbishop on a mission of love

Having discovered the gardens, love compels you to action.

It's not a complicated choice.

You can't know inner serenity while watching others

suffering and choosing to do nothing to help.

My screen images for MMMM are love, goodness, truth, justice, mercy, forgiveness and hope.

Jesus appears to be someone who had found his way to the garden. He loved and helped others and urged us to love.

There are reports that he loved lepers, sex workers, criminals and those despised by others.

He chose ordinary working people to help him.

He accommodated their faults.

Even when he was being killed, the reports say he was kind to the man dying next to him.

Even though Jesus' choice to die was misguided, and shocked and frightened his followers, they had been so impressed with his love, they carried on speaking about him.

Unfortunately this simple experience of love was transformed into an ugly religious system, rank with power and politics, epitomised in a title like 'Archbishop'.

However, having bucked at the Anglican Church in which I found myself trapped, I began ministering independently, like Jesus did, outside the status quo. I was consecrated a bishop to be able to confound the establishment and was elected Archbishop by the clerics with whom I shared a common vision of building inclusive loving community.

I have no interest in the title 'Archbishop' other than it providing a platform to ridicule its pretentiousness and to lay siege to the power systems it has spawned.

The approach from paradise

Having found the gardens of paradise – titles, vestments, systems, rituals, religions, dogmas and doctrines are all insignificant and I am quite happy to discard them.

I heard of Jesus along my life's journey. I was impressed by his life-changing love.

I warmed to the rebellious spirit he displayed, snubbing the religious leaders, creating leaders out of labourers and doing religion in a people-centred way.

I counted myself in.

I was 'processed', did my stint as a Vicar and after 12 years managed to escape.

*H*aving been set on love's path by meeting Jesus, I have met since so many other travellers sharing the same road, from every faith, philosophy, culture and race, some religious and many not.

And as an Archbishop?

As an Archbishop I can resist the wrecking tactics of rotten church while being free, like Jesus, to love.

As an Archbishop I can try and encourage a model community to grow unlike any other at the moment that has no walls, no excluding boundaries and is open to everyone in the spirit of love. One jigsaw piece, one thread, with the ability to fit or weave perfectly with all others. If such an approach is replicated in every gathering of people, whatever their interest or activity, then we will have begun to create the means by which all our separate expressions of humanity can integrate into one idyllic whole in which everyone plays their critical part.

As an Archbishop I can try and rescue those trapped within religious straightjackets and liberate them to fly in the slipstream of love. I can endeavour to consecrate further bishops and ordain further priests, not to be stooges of a system but creative, inventive, imaginative, original and ingenious bearers of love to a needy world.

However, all these things can be done without being an archbishop, bishop, priest or having any such title. In fact the titles often intrude, contaminate and prevent the flow of authentic pure love and that is why I sit loosely to my title and would happily relinquish it.

Love is paramount

MMMM, if there is a MMMM, she/he/? can only, in my perception, be the ultimate expression of love.

Ours is to love.

My life's work is to learn how to love.

I am first and foremost a human being.

My name is not Archbishop.

It is Jonathan.

I share with all other humans the process by which others give a child the sound by which she or he will be known. It is possible to change it but I am familiar with my own and it causes no offence, so I use it.

How people view me or refer to me otherwise, and by what different names they call me or what titles they afford me is of little significance, other than for the information it provides about them.

Who I am, why I am, what I am remain intriguing mysteries.

What I do is for me to decide and for me to be responsible and accountable.

My choice is to love, because love alone makes any sense.

This defines me.

I am a child of the world, no different from and one with all others, here to play my part as best I can to benefit others and the world and myself.

I long for us all to walk and work together.

Love is supreme

Every person craves love.

My role as a person and as a minister is to interpret everything that is external as of secondary importance to love. The test of every choice and every action is whether it is motivated by love, suffused with love, planned and prepared in love, expressive of love and aspiring to love.

Nothing precedes love in importance.

Nothing competes with love in significance.

Nothing surpasses love in its ability to create, cherish and nurture life.

I am content, therefore, to be a kaleidoscope of humanity, available to everyone, inspired by every good and gracious person from every faith, race and culture.

I am comfortable with leading any ritual, community event or service using uplifting material from any tradition or source. I am at ease wearing any form of vestment, costume, uniform or attire that is appropriate and meaningful to the occasion or the participants. I am at peace when I use the language, the symbols and the approach that brings comfort and compassion to those to whom I am ministering.

All these external matters are interchangeable as long as the human hearts choosing them experience love.

Love is ultimate

It is love that creates the rainbow bridge across every human heart that has ever existed and ever will that promises us true community and the unity of purpose and life from which all good things come.

It is love that will lead us away from conflict and destruction towards the paradise we seek.

I am eager to serve and help any person in the world and to regard them as my own.

I am prepared when I die to be responsible for everything I have done and the choices I have made and to allow my life to be assessed by the highest authority.

Love.

Chapter 24

Handing Spirituality Back to the People

Having managed to escape from the Church of England's clutches and having established myself as a cleric, working independently, I set about trying to explore and experiment with offering ministry in a flexible and accessible manner in tune with modern living and choices.

It gave me a chance to cross the boundaries, rules and requirements that the religious systems had spawned to protect their own interests and serve their own agendas.

I had long been affronted by the prejudice and discrimination practiced routinely by the Anglican Church; now I had the chance to offer something very different.

Equal marriage

In 1994, I was the first cleric to advertise, in Gay Times and Diva, my willingness to perform marriage ceremonies for gay and lesbian couples. I became inundated with requests and travelled across the UK and abroad witnessing family and friends gathering to celebrate the weddings of their LGBT loved ones.

In 2001, I performed the first gay wedding on the prime time 'This Morning' – Richard and Judy's TV show. It was Valentine's Day. The item was regarded as one of the 20 most controversial TV broadcasts and the Daily Mail was scathing in its reporting. I sued Associated Newspapers and spent the next two and a half years in litigation culminating in a successful outcome. My integrity, the integrity of our church, our holy orders and our ministry were upheld, I had to pay no costs at all and part of my costs were covered.

I was delighted to be able to offer gay and lesbian couples exactly the same respect and approach to the arrangement of their marriages as I did heterosexual couples.

Over the years I have taken thousands of weddings and have had the joy of being asked to baptise the children of some of the gay and lesbian couples.

I had a dream that one day the law would catch up and legalise equal marriage!

At the same time that the large churches were discriminating against gay and lesbian couples, they were also discriminating against co-habiting and divorced couples or those couples who weren't baptised or who didn't attend church regularly.

Additionally, the churches regarded weddings as a chance to use their buildings and charge for their bells, heating, choir and organist as well as the cleric. Couples had a choice of either the registry office or church.

Then changes in the law allowed the registry office wedding to be conducted in licensed premises, giving a greater and more attractive range of venues and choice to the couples. However, the Church of England remained rigid about having to use their church buildings and having to use only the liturgies approved by Synod.

In stark contrast to this, I advertised my willingness to celebrate love and provide marriage ceremonies to everyone, irrespective of their background, in any location of their choosing, inside or out, licensed or not and using the words chosen by the couple. I developed a comprehensive resource book of words from which the couple could choose (reproduced later in this book) or they could write their own.

I conducted weddings on beaches, hilltops, under water, in forests, planes, speedboats, over the Internet, on Wild West ranches, in Moroccan palaces, gardens, homes, National Trust Estates, Zoos, on TV, in castles, chapels, stone circles and shrines. I conducted weddings all over the UK, in Ireland, Spain, Ibiza, Minorca, Marrakech, Crete, Monaco and France.

I have swum down the aisle and danced down the aisle, worn

gold brocade robes and Hawaiian shirts. I have married men and men, women and women, women who once were men and men who once were women and men and women! I have married women in trousers and trainers and men in full bridal attire. I have married the rich and the poor, in opulence and simplicity, celebrities and the rest; I have even married two dogs in a chapel in Leicestershire!

Some may choose to be sceptical, even to mock, but all of the ceremonies celebrated love, brought joy to all involved and consolidated respectful and stable attitudes and relationships within society.

Love is our highest and our best and must never be constrained or damaged by law.

Baptisms, christenings and celebrating the birth and naming of a child

Since 1994, a social revolution has taken place quietly, unassumingly, but that has brought about considerable change.

It was the *case* that the denominational churches had a stranglehold over how the celebration of the birth of a child, in baptism or thanksgiving, could be provided.

Families were subject to invasive requirements that involved six months of church attendance, the appointment of church approved Godparents and attendance at a training course or house group.

Discrimination was rife against single mothers and single fathers, against the divorced, those co-habiting and those who did not attend church.

If their local parish rejected their request and they enquired at another church nearby or with which they had connection, the priest would always consult with their parish priest first and if bidden to do so, turn them away also.

So in 1994, I began to advertise my willingness to provide baptism or thanksgiving or naming services in any location and venue, even at home or in the garden of the family. Suddenly families had a choice that respected their circumstances and beliefs.

I appeared on This Morning, Littlejohn, Esther, Stapleton, Trisha, Vanessa, National Geographic and the History Channel. Jimmy Young and Libby Purves interviewed me on their Radio shows. I was featured on BBC, ITV and Sky News. Articles appeared widely in the national press and popular magazines.

My approach was welcomed overwhel*m*ingly by the public.

I was inundated with interest and have carried out subsequently thousands of home and other baptisms all over the UK

On the summit of Mount Snowdon, in the waters off Monaco, in a circus ring, in forests, by rivers and in golf clubs, in pubs, clubs, hotels and country estates, in flats, terraced houses and mansions, for celebrities, sports stars, politicians and the rest of us, in the Houses of Parliament and in people's home gardens.

It has been a joy to see families freed to be able to celebrate the lives of their children as they wish without the overbearing intrusion of church and regulation.

Now there are many independent practitioners offering similar services and families are able to create a bespoke ceremony for their children.

Personal funerals, memorials and celebration of life services

A bereaved family are often not in any condition to be able to consider their options nor empowered to find out the best way to arrange a funeral.

Unfortunately most undertakers still adopt a default position of using the local Anglican cleric, even if the person was not a regular church attendee and only nominally Church of England, by which 'Christian' is meant invariably.

Instead of having a service that honours their loved one, a family is subjected to nonsensical prayers and an alien liturgy.

Increasingly there are numerous alternative celebrants and families are growing wise to ask for one of these instead.

The essential heart of any funeral must be the words spoken in description, thanks, memory and celebration of the bereaved. The religious content, if any, must be kept to a minimum and used purely to provide comfort and hope to the bereaved.

I ensure the wishes of the family are respected, even down to what I wear. I have taken funerals in football shirts, Hawaiian shirts, gold brocade vestments and in jeans. I have taken them beside lakes, in forests, on hilltops and at sea, in chapels and churches, in cemeteries and graveyards, in hotels and people's front rooms. I have blown bubbles, danced and toasted the deceased with whisky. I have sung and chanted, taken religious and non-religious services, offered Jewish, Muslim, Hindu, Buddhist prayers as well as Christian ones.

I have held the hands of the dying, sung them hymns, songs and re*ad* soothing words, accompanied them to the point of death. I have anointed them with oil and held vigil with them through the night. I have garlanded their deathbeds with flowers.

I have surrounded their grave plots with roses, draped the gravesides in white silk and covered the bare earth, awaiting the coffin and then the coffin itself with fragrant rose petals of many colours.

I have prepared the ground for cremated remains, making a bed of carnations upon which the ash can fall, lovingly poured over the hands of loved ones, covered then by more flowers and sealed with fresh earth formed and shaped as a heart and embellished again with flower petals to define the heart's contours.

I have sought to make these profound moments of farewell uplifting, sensitive beautiful and expressive of the family's hopes.

Mass – Holy Communion

Having handed back the practice of celebrating love and marriage, birth and baptism and death and burial to families, it was important to hand back the most guarded sacrament of all. The sacrament imprisoned behind steel doors and locks on altars and in churches across the world.

The 'Body' and 'Blood' of Christ symbolised in wafer bread and wine are at the heart of Christian worship and power.

At first, I celebrated Mass on the streets in Leicester Square, London and in Trafalgar Square and distributed the mass to the central London street dwellers and the sex workers throughout Soho, knocking on the doors of the brothels and distributing the Mass to the maids and workers inside.

I celebrated the Mass on hilltops, beaches, boats and canals; in front rooms, trains and hotels, but it became apparent that these individual acts of worship were of limited scope and effect and something with greater reach was required.

Post the Host was the outcome. Literally consecrating the bread and wine in a Eucharistic service and then making it available by post to anyone who wished to receive or distribute the sacrament.

When Post the Host was launched, there were articles in the press in this country and across the world, as well as Europe-wide TV coverage. It was a sensational development. Roman Catholic priests from Italy and England visited my home, Bishop's Haven in Welling. Requests for the sacrament were received from America, Germany, Canada, France, Holland, Italy, Croatia, Finland, New Zealand and across the United Kingdom.

I developed various Mass liturgies posted on YouTube to suit different approaches and tastes, including an inclusive Mass, a radical Mass and the most viewed, a street Mass. I emphasised also that no priest or minister was necessary and any person could consecrate the bread and the wine, should they wish.

I also took the sacrament to distribute on the streets of central London, in Trafalgar Square and outside Westminster Cathedral.

In one interesting setting, I positioned myself outside

Westminster Abbey, amongst the hawkers selling 'official Westminster Abbey merchandise', and by a sign setting out the high charges for admittance to the abbey.

I had a sign too, the only one offering something for free – the Body and Blood of Christ. Many approached me to receive. Many found themselves in tears, to happen unexpectedly upon an experience of receiving Jesus in the street, on their holiday, as a tourist, a shopper or on their way to work.

At Communion services, I encouraged people receiving Communion to take a handful of consecrated wafer breads to hand out to strangers on their way home and share with family, friends and the housebound.

Holy Orders

The last great power kept under tight security in the church is the ability to transmit Holy Orders – to ordain a deacon, priest or consecrate a bishop.

These functions are reserved to the episcopate, the bishops.

In 2000, I was consecrated a bishop and was, thereby, empowered with the grace and faculty to grow the church, according to the apostolic tradition.

It meant that instead of being trapped as a rebel, a mere individual, within a male system of clericature, which remained controlled by the institution, I was able to set about building a new expression of church.

I wanted to ordain irrespective of gender, sexual orientation, disability, social class, background, race or any other irrelevant, invidious and divisive categorisation.

I wanted to remove the artificial obstacles to ordination placed to screen out applicants that while worthy, did not fit the social type desired by the denominational moguls.

Over the last decades I have ordained deacons and priests of every sort and consecrated bishops likewise: Men and women, homosexual and heterosexual, formally educated and not, abled and disabled or 'differently abled' as I prefer to describe them, 'working class' and 'middle class', of different races and skin tones, of different backgrounds and nationalities.

Now there are clerics commissioned to minister inclusively and with unconditional love to all people, spreading across the world.

Part V

Chapter 25

Jade Goody's Wedding

I was in Tenerife, on holiday with my family, when I was asked to conduct Jade's wedding blessing. We had been following her plight in the papers. I flew home for five days to take the wedding and then returned to Tenerife.

It seemed that the entire world was gripped by Jade's struggle. Her courage in the face of impending death, her love for her boys, her relationship with the media and her desire to marry Jack had all combined to provide a compelling and tragic drama.

News outlets provided saturated coverage of every development and the media set up camp outside her home.

The chaos

I found my visit to Jade's home disturbing. It was teeming with activity. Numerous people whose lives had become absorbed into Jade's world filled the rooms. These were not family or close friends, but advisors, media staff, PR helpers, agency staff and OK journalists to mention a few.

The staff from the registry office arrived.

Then doctors and nurses and medical practitioners began congregating. Apparently they were going to hold a case meeting to review Jade's home care and medication. I suspected that the review was being held at Jade's home due to her fame, everyone wanted to share in it. By the time the meeting began there were around 10 health professionals in attendance.

Meanwhile Jade was asleep in her bedroom.

She awoke into this mayhem.

An emaciated, weak and very forlorn Jade was wheeled into the room. She was dazed and uncertain. A minder introduced the registrars to her and they set about arranging the civil wedding.

The preparation

There were so many people who 'wanted to see Jade' and consume what was left of her time on earth that I felt embarrassed to be one of those waiting in the queue, although I reassured myself that I had been asked to visit her home.

When I was finally led into the room where she and Jack were lying together and our time began, the door burst open and a nurse entered informing Jade that her case review was about to begin and didn't she want to be there!

It felt a macabre intrusion, petitioning the dying star to perform by her presence for the gathered health practitioners. She declined wisely with a wistful look.

Of course the cameras had followed my entry into the room. Every aspect of Jade's demise was for sale. The world was her companion.

Intimacy

I wanted to try and remain separate from this great Jade roadshow with all its groupies and connect with what was real at the heart of the story.

Here was a young woman, terrified of dying, horrified at the thought of leaving her boys and clinging on to the man who was offering her love.

I asked how they had met, what they had felt when they first set eyes upon each other, what attracted them in those first kindling moments, how they arranged their first date and where it happened, why they loved each other and what they appreciated about each other.

It was touching to watch Jade emerge from the horror of her illness. She relaxed, her face began to shine, she laughed, and they giggled together and teased one another. Playfully they spoke about their love and experiences and together we found words for the wedding blessing that they felt expressed their feelings for each other.

Prayer

I asked if they wanted me to pray with them.

Suddenly the intimacy we had shared had led us to an even greater connection. It was the first time the cameras were banished. Everyone was asked to leave. The groupies, advisors, camera crew all scuttled away, the door closed and Jack, Jade and I were alone in the presence of the mystery.

Tranquillity suffused the room. The crazy antics and manic activity in the house were tamed. The terrors being faced were calmed in the presence of the love that flowed within the room. Those moments provided an oasis.

I held Jade and Jack's hands and began to speak some words of prayer.

Jade's face was aglow.

She looked so peaceful. As though she had glimpsed something that had re-assured her, strengthened and invigorated her.

Later she would comment how special and awesome that time had been.

The wedding day

The Jade that left the house that day was transformed. Her energy levels were high, her spirit on fire and her eagerness for the wedding immense.

There was so much to do and Jade remained indefatigable.

It was as though the wedding was to be the consummation of her life.

She radiated joy. She relished being surrounded by all those she loved and who loved her. She delighted in the extraordinary generosity of all those who had offered their services and skills to achieve the wedding of a lifetime.

Her beauty that day was dazzling.

Its sublime nature arose from the juxtaposition of hope in the presence of despair, intimacy on the threshold of separation and of course life on the brink of death. The pathos expressed most poignantly in the lives of two wide-eyed boys caught up in a drama about which they knew so little.

The wedding blessing

Family and friends were mesmerised as Jade walked down the aisle, her head shining and her body slight, yet filling the room with her presence and energy.

Unsurprisingly she was nervous, but I began to refer to the simple stories of their fledging love…

'It was a casual look across a nightclub (wasn't it Jack)… a meandering walk to a piano bar and jugs of drink (you told me Jade)…. And that special song…'

I spoke of the innocent happiness they had found together…

'Just those fragile and whimsical happenings that let stardust settle upon your two hearts to change your world'.

Soon everything else had faded – her anxiety, her dying, the cameras, the celebrity.

'And so, not for you both, on earth alone do you wish this wedding to be blessed, but in heaven too… Then hush awhile, let's create that rainbow bridge – let's cut through with a subtle knife by prayer, by grace, to that other world… oh always so near, radiant with light, brimming with love, a paradise awaiting…'

I began to sing:

'Turn your eyes upon Jesus, look full in his wonderful face. And the things of earth will grow strangely dim, in the light of his glory and grace…'

Jade's face was serene and tranquil.

Words of love

I spoke the following words on their behalf.

'I love you ever my Jack and without reserve… the more I have known you my Jade, the more I have loved you… when I see you my Jack, then I feel well again. When you open your eyes, my body is whole again…'

I reminded them of one sentiment they had shared with me, that spoke eloquently of their love – 'When we are with each other, we feel completely safe'.

'Together, it is as though the half of you has met the whole, as though that elusive missing part has been discovered, as though at last you have found your way home.'

The reading for the service was poignant.

'The life that I have is all that I have and the life that I have is yours. The love that I have of the life that I have is yours and yours and yours.

A sleep I shall have, a rest I shall have, yet death it will be but a pause.

For the peace of my years in the long green grass will be yours and yours and yours'.

An oasis

I reminded them of the time we had shared when I had seen them gaze at one another, be vulnerable and tender. They had giggled, teased one another and been cheeky. Their deep love was vivid and tangible.

'So let this place' I suggested 'become an oasis, a mountain height, a sacred space, a healing garden, a songbird's theme within which now to give your hearts.'

From all the vows I had shown them, they had chosen vows that I had written.

Jack said to Jade:

'No one has touched my life like you.
No one can compare with you
No one else has made my heart leap and my soul dance
Nor set my mind alight with joy.
In your presence I have found my rest, my home and my self.
In your arms I have known such peace.

Today I give myself to you.
I am yours *an*d ever shall it be.
Jade said to Jack:
You are so handsome to me
You are my life, my light, my hope and my joy.
I will treasure you. I will cherish you.
I will be utterly devoted to you
Through the laughter and the tears
Through the darkness and the light
I will be your eternal love
Your constant companion, your closest friend
Pledging to you my deepest commitment
And this is my solemn vow'.

The lighting of the wedding candle

After giving the rings they lit a lifetime candle…

I invited them to conceive of the rekindling of the candle every anniversary.

'…a hand on earth… a hand from heaven… one light… one everlasting love.'

I ended the service with words that encompassed the present and future.

'…May each sunset harbour the promise of another day, on this or a more golden shore… for your love will take you beyond our borders, across unknown continents, to whole new worlds beyond…'

The photograph of the blessing in OK magazine portrayed vividly Jade's profound happiness.

Throughout the day her smile filled every moment. Soaring above the pain and discomfort, she wove her affection and bright personality from table to table and guest to guest.

Always cheeky

After the service, when we left the guests for a while so Jade could rest, her vivacious spirit was irrepressible. She wanted a photograph with me. The photographer obliged and took some more formal ones. However, she wanted a cheeky one and posed with one leg kicked back and her arms raised, looking back over her shoulder at me.

She was the most possessed, charming, energetic and happy bride who exulted in every second of the day.

I can see her face now, as the long day culminated in a firework display, sitting with Jack and her beloved boys, gazing up at the kaleidoscopic sky, bathed in love on earth and heaven bound.

Chapter 26

Jade Goody's Death

As if the dying of a young mother was not tragedy enough, her last breath being taken on Mother's Day intensified the poignancy.

Her boys had been her life. They were not with her during those last hours. Camped outside her home were the world's media and hundreds of the public, keeping vigil.

News of her death headlined everywhere and the media machine descended on me, snatching me into a scrambled itinerary for broadcasts from one studio to another.

I adopted a phrase that she was the 'Princess from Bermondsey and a Saint from Upshire'.

A Saint?

Some acerbic commentators were quick to react scornfully to the idea that she could be regarded as a saint.

Their cynicism illustrated the divide between modern perceptions and church history.

I was comparing Jade with many who the church have declared to be saints, whose lives were chequered or unknown but who had come to faith, often in the eye of peril and who in their last breaths and choices had achieved something remarkable. Jade fitted amply such a profile.

Simple faith

Jade could not conceive of being separated from her boys and this motivated her to turn to her faith and have her boys baptised. She drew comfort from the hope that she would be able to watch over them from heaven and one day be re-united with them.

Thus strengthened, she laughed in the face of death and squeezed every last drop of possibility from her remaining days. Refusing to choose privacy, even when emaciated and bald, she took her victory parade for all to see, as the conqueror of death's shadows.

Her plight highlighted the importance of testing for cervical cancer and thousands of women attended clinics.

Her charitable work had alleviated the suffering of poor children in India.

She emerged from a fragile background with little formal education, yet she displayed a keen intelligence.

She gave herself vulnerably to the public who came to love her and appreciate her warm, real and at times shocking humanity.

The burial ground

The established church showed no interest in her in life, only in so much as they could capitalise on her fame in death.

Jade had said she wanted me to baptise the children but she wanted desperately also to be buried in the churchyard of St John's Church, Buckhurst Hill, near Jack's home.

With that in mind she approached St John's in the mistaken belief that if they baptised the children, they would allow her to be buried in the graveyard of the church.

The Church of England's media machine cranked into overdrive and issued press releases about the baptism.

The sting in the tail wasn't revealed until later. The churchyard was full and Jade would have to be buried elsewhere.

The funeral

Thankfully most of the funeral contained personal contributions from those who knew and loved Jade and the mandatory religious text was kept to the minimum, delivered in a typically 'Anglican' sterile and disinterested tone.

The real service and liturgy was found in the conversations of the thousands who lined the streets outside, who *re*spected and loved Jade.

Before and after the service I distributed cards with Jade's photograph on the front and a prayer I had written on the back:

Dear God of Love

Thank you for Jade.

Bless her in Paradise

Our brightest star.

Be with Jackiey, Jack, Bobby and Freddy

And all her family and friends in their grief.

Comfort all those who mourn

And may the example of Jade's courage in adversity, humour in the face of suffering and sheer love of life.

Turn our sorrow into joy and our tears into laughter.

Amen.

I gave one to a police constable who was so moved that they have since applied to be ordained.

The wake

Jade's Mum had asked me to lead a private service of prayer, just for the family and friends, at the gathering after the funeral.

The sky was blue and the horizons far as I said…

'One enduring memory I have of my time with Jade was after we had prayed together.

I opened my eyes and her eyes were still closed with her face upturned. She looked so serene and her face was shining like an angel's.

She was confident of heaven.

We've just said goodbye to Jade's poorly body, for which she has no further use.

But she's not dead and we've not left her at the cemetery and these balloons are for her.

Beautiful Jade, thank you for all you've given us,

Your love and laughter

and the magic you've woven, as golden thread, into all our lives.

Now your spirit is free,
You've soared high through the wide blue expanse of sky
Into the sun's warmth and the wind's breath
Past the dance of the stars and the planets.
You've crossed the bridge of dreams,
Been reclothed in a new body and fallen
Into the arms of loved ones waiting upon that golden shore
You're safe
in paradise
and watching with us now.
And oh, how we miss you,
But our love is ever with you
And we know that we will see you, hold you and be together with you again.
So until that halcyon day, our eyes will caress you by night, our 'brightest star'
Our memories will warm us by day.
And upon these balloons, we've written our tear-stained jottings
That express our heartfelt and eternal love for you.
They bear the kisses of our love to you in heaven
as now we release them'.

The legacy

I cherish Jade's memory.

I regard her as a true saint. Not a plaster cast cobwebbed historical figure that the church knows nothing about, except a few scraps of legend upon which they have hung a sainthood.

No. Jade was a real flesh and blood saint, who stripped in the big brother house for the world to see, and swore and said racist things for which she had the humility to apologise but she also brought humour, hope, courage, life and inspiration to countless thousands across the world.

I am still asked about Jade by members of the public. They speak of her with an enduring affection and respect. She lives on as a bright and positive memory for them.

For someone who loves her and would appreciate holding something significant she held and used on her wedding day, I am offering to give away the glass candlesticks she held and used to light her wedding candle.

I have throughout the book placed a verse from a poem and a text reference, hidden, using a pattern, within the text. Anyone who finds them can email them to me, plus who wrote the poem and the remaining verses, at:

bishopjonathanblake@ntlworld.com

or text me on:

07767 687711

to claim the candlesticks.

Then you can use them to cherish her memory forever.

When someone has correctly sent me the set of words and the candlesticks have been claimed, I will place an announcement to this effect on the blog on my web site:

www.bishopjonathanblake.com.

Part VI

Chapter 27

In Conclusion

One life…
We have but one life.
One short moment.
One chance to play our part.
One opportunity to choose.
Others would steal it gladly, squander it, debase it.
Others would control it, manipulate and usurp it.
But it is ours.
Given to us.
Protect it.
From Gods and from earthlings.
From clerics and from religionists.
From philosophies and fantasies.
From mediums and magic.
Take charge. Be responsible.
Know that we have evolved into the most advanced life form known.
Every day is unique. An empty page.
Consider well our words.
Our direction.
Our aims.
Our hopes.
Each day we carve indelibly the stuff of life.
We become.
Our identity is revealed.
Our life is known.
We have but this one life.
Make it beautiful.
Make it count.
Make it good.

Part VII

Chapter 28

Inclusive Words and Acts for Uniting the World

As part of an exploration in how to 'originate' instead of worship, I wanted to offer these resources, to be used personally or with others, spoken or sung, by one person or together.

They are not religious.

They do not assu*me* a religious approach.

They are human expressions that build bridges across our experiences, celebrating wonder, harnessing resources, identifying apsirations and giving voice to our thoughts and feelings.

A celebration of life

Come let us sing out to Life

Let us exult in the strength of all that saves us

Let us come before creation with thanksgiving and cry out joyfully in songs of praise.

For our world is a great world, and a great planet above all planets.

In nature's gift are all the corners of the earth, the high hills, the sea

And the dry land moulded for our habitation.

Come, let us worship and revere the mystery of life and kneel in humility before the

glory of creation.

For we have been given life; we are people of the earth and enjoy the beauty of this

world's pastures.

If only we would hear Love's voice, for Love comes to judge the earth.

Love shall judge us all with righteousness and truth.

Glory to all that creates, redeems and inspires,
Now and forever.

An act of contrition

We have offended our neighbours and ourselves
We have wounded love's grace
We have fallen short of our best.
We are sorry and ashamed.
May we experience forgiveness
And may we strive anew
To walk as children of the light.

Thanksgiving

Glory to Love in the purest
And peace to all forms of life
We praise
We bless
We adore
We glorify
We give thanks for all that is good
Love, justice, truth and peace
Kindness and mercy
Good people, from all ages
Faiths and cultures
Our inspiration and our light
Who take away the wrongs of the world
Embolden us
Who take away the evil of the world
Guide us
Who are held in the greatest respect
Inspire us
For you are to be revered
Honoured and remembered
Shining lights, urging goodness on

Through every generation.

An act of unity and solidarity

We are alive. We are children of the earth. We lift our hearts in thanks and praise.
We have discovered the grace of Love. We have seen acts of kindness and goodness.
We have witnessed the inspiring and heroic actions of others.
We respect those who have played their part in seeking to establish a world of justice and peace.
We bow our heads in honour of the brave and the true.
Praise, respect, glory and honour be to those who have given their best and offered their all.
We give thanks for every good thing that we have received
For hope in times of despair
For light in seasons of darkness
For comfort in the valley of suffering
We give thanks for those who reach out to help and to rescue
The lost and the lonely
The poor and the homeless
The broken and the bereaved
As we gather together in the spirit of friendship and love
And pledge ourselves to work tirelessly for a better world
We remember all those who have suffered and suffer for the Cause of righteousness.
We remember all those who have opened wide their hearts and sacrificed their lives
Who have been tortured, imprisoned and murdered for noble ends
whose flesh has been torn and whose blood has been spilt
that others might taste a sweeter future and know a brighter end.
We remember all those who have gathered with their family and

friends before their ordeal unfolded; who broke bread and who
drank in affection and solidarity.
In taking the bread and tearing it; in lifting the red juice and pouring it, we join with them, partaking of their plight, identifying
with their suffering, pledging our commitment to work to realise
their dreams, that their suffering may not be in vain.
In sharing together the bread and the juice we are nourished by
their example and become one with them in the struggle of all people to change this world for the better.
Therefore, with this bread and this juice
we commemorate the suffering of the innocent.
May this meal of memories and this food and drink of love
open our eyes and set our hearts on fire
to unite with everyone that right may prevail.
(The bread and juice of life and love are shared)

A declaration of hope and intent

May Love be revered
May Unity come
Good will be done
That earth may evolve into heaven
May we work hard today for our daily bread
And may our sins be forgiven
As we forgive those
Who have sinned against us
And may we not fall into temptation
But be delivered from evil
For we believe in justice, truth and peace
For ever *and* ever

A statement of resolve

Nothing need ever defeat us, discourage or deter us.

Strengthened by love's resolve, the solidarity of the suffering and the

friendship of all those involved in the quest to achieve

peace and justice, we will proceed with unlimited reserves of hope,

love and forgiveness to make the dream of universal happiness and

freedom come true and may all that is good come to our

aid.

Chapter 29

Words for a Marriage Ceremony for Any Two People

The Preface

In the name of Love; creative, redemptive and life-giving. Bless us today.

May love and peace and happiness fill you and surround you.

Words of love

Where, O where do I begin, to tell you how much I love you; how much you've changed my life; how much I long to be with you?

I never realised what love was – until I met you.

I want only to walk beside you; to pass through this world beside you; to fulfil my destiny beside you.

You are the rock upon which I want to build my life, my future and my all.

For the couple

You stand together, on the threshold of a myriad of dreams and hopes; for love has brought you, bright-eyed and eager, to this place.

Today, you enter the most sacred place within the land of love. A garden reserved for those who have found their heart's delight and their soul's awakening.

The Introduction

(Names would be inserted to personalise the text and only some of the paragraphs would be selected)

Thank you for love. The love which found us when we were alone, warmed us when we were cold, soothed us when hurting and healed us when broken. Thank you for the love, which has breathed new life within us, shone new light upon us and graced each day with hope.

We have come together to witness this marriage. We are their friends and their family. We value them and are with them today as they set out on this great adventure.

They have completed the legal formalities for marriage but for them this is what is necessary to make their marriage complete, when surrounded by those they love they make their vows to one another and receive our blessing.

They come from different families, they are different people, and they have walked different paths. But in a mysterious way, all the steps they have taken have led them to the wonder of this moment.

Love from their parents and grandparents; love from their brothers and sisters, love from their family and friends; this love, richly, fully, freely given has helped make them what they are today and enabled them to offer the gift of their unique lives to each other.

Today we celebrate the discovery and the nurturing of their special love for each other and the way it has further enriched their lives and we look forward with them to all the promise that the future holds.

Marriage is the promise of hope between two people who love each other, who trust that love, who honour one another as individuals and who wish to share their future together.

It enables two separate people to share their desires, longings, dreams and memories, their joys and their laughter. It enables them to help each other through times of uncertainty and provides them with the encouragement to risk more and thus to gain more.

When we love, we see things other people cannot. We see beneath the surface and observe that which others may not. To see with loving eyes is to know an inner beauty, and to be loved is to be seen and known as we are known to no other.

When we love we are loved and when we are loved we love. Love gives birth to love and hope and trust and joy. Love sets us free to be ourselves. Love gives us wings with which to fly. Love is the sunlight, which warms our hearts and lives. It is this beautiful love, which the couple have discovered, which has changed their lives, which has brought them to this moment.

In marriage, two people embark upon a journey that has no ending, only an infinite number of beginnings. They face the mystery of the future and all that awaits them. The years will change them, but as a family is bonded eternally together, parent to child, sister to brother, so partner to partner. Love allows for no separation.

As such the pathways of love are exacting as well as bountiful. This day history shall record the joining together of two lives, two families, and two groups of friends. There is nothing in all the delights and deceits of this world that can ever erase this bond.

Even if in the future the law, shall, out of necessity, name the bond as broken, the truth is forever lodged within the heart of creation that those united this day were joined forever. They may become estranged, as tragically happens within families, but they shall forever remain a part of that family's history.

Furthermore, those who are blessed by love's greatest miracle and so bear children into this world must know that the coloured threads of two families are woven into their creation. By their birth an irrevocable union has been made. However far apart the parents may travel from each other, they will always meet again at the bridge of their children's lives.

As such, those bonded in love do well to heed the wisdom of the ages: that they tend to one another as to no other, that there is no escaping the covenant made in marriage and through the birth of children, that there is no relationship on earth comparable to the one shared with your wedded partner and that no one can ever take their place.

Those who have already been married bear in their hearts the pain they have known and the wisdom they have gained through all that has been. Today, knowing from whence they have come and what is theirs to do, they set their face towards a new path and a new future.

Their children are a supremely important part of the future and they will always cherish them and be there for them.

There are *few* things that can so damage a soul as a love lost or broken. For someone to suffer that shattering, to collect the broken shards of their life and to restore themselves sufficiently to respond to love's sweet presence is a marvellous thing.

Generous life affords to every one of us so many chances, so much mercy and so much hope. That hope, effervescent within us, is the keeper of our souls. How grateful are they that through everything and despite everything they have found one another. In one another, their treasure has at last been discovered and their dreams fulfilled. Nothing or no one will ever take them from each other.

In marriage, you are joined together, and together you shall be for evermore.

In marriage, two people discover every contour of their partner's soul and being and every emotion is available to be experienced. They may well love, hate, like or despise each other. They may be proud of, then ashamed, have dreams fulfilled, and then dashed, be excited, then bored, be stretched and limited. They may feel set free then imprisoned, they may rage, laugh, weep and dance all with the one they love, because this is love.

Not the sentimental, transitory, and oftentimes fickle love of early passion, of fiction and of fantasy.

True love is often a messy, complicated happening, with struggles, heartaches, confusions and uncertainties; but what is known by those who have faced all, endured all and stood the test of time, is that *the* jewel beyond price, the fulfilment beyond description and the security beyond knowledge is found by those who have offered to each other an unconditional love, who have been willing to cope with and face, anything and everything together, and who are thus able to accompany one another onwards as closest friends.

In a few moments we shall be present as this great covenant of love is enacted before us. They will affirm their choice and desire to enter the hallowed realm of marriage. They will speak their solemn words of promise and commitment. A new family will be born in our midst and a profound happiness will bless us all.

Readings may be inserted here and then a further selection of the following paragraphs

Marriage expresses the strength of love and devotion enjoyed by two people whose lives have become woven together. Their appreciation of one another and the confidence they have in their relationship brings them to this important step. Our horizons always contain mystery but marriage enables our journey onwards to be warmed and enriched by the presence of another, in whom we invest our trust, our hope, and our life.

You believe in a relationship based on openness in which each will love, honour and treasure the other, remaining devoted companions for all your days. Listening and laughing, caring and sharing, you wish to live your lives to the full, enabling one another through encouragement and sensitive words.

Marriage enables two people to discover each other as never before; to journey towards the centre of each other's soul, mind, heart and body; to be confronted by places of brokenness; to wound and be wounded, just as to discover rich sources of life, to create and be recreated.

There exist within marriage some of our greatest emotional and spiritual possibilities. We marry not only to be loved and feel secure, to come home to our loved one and have our needs met; we marry also to enhance our capacity to love, to nurture, to give and forgive, to heal and to inspire.

When we love we exercise our choice. Being quite capable of living without each other, two people yet choose to live together; and in that choosing, to entertain the hope of something more wonderful being created through the weaving of the coloured threads of their lives.

When you love someone, you do not feel love for him or her all the time, in exactly the same way, from moment to moment. We have so little faith in the ebb and flow of life, of love, of relationships. We leap at the flow of the tide and resist in terror its ebb. We are afraid it will never return. We insist on permanency, on duration, on continuity; when the only continuity possible, in life as in love, is in growth, in fluidity – in freedom, in the sense that dancers are free, barely touching as they pass, but partners in the same pattern.

The only real security in a relationship is not in owning or possessing, not in demanding or expecting, not looking back to what was in nostalgia, nor forward to what might be in dread or anticipation, but living in the present moment. Relationships are like islands, joined yet interrupted by the sea, continually visited and yet also abandoned by the tides.

A marriage is not a prison but a wide-open space; not a set of chains but a path to freedom; maintaining that liberty is the essence of love. It will be witness to each partner's choices and changes, the mistakes and the glory. It can cause the heart to bleed and the soul to despair but such suffering blended with joy and fermented over the years creates love's vintage wine that brings delight.

A good family watches with each other through all the changing scenes of life, and holds within its embrace the bruises and the benefits of its loved ones. In marriage a new family is born. Your vows will commission you, to be so devoted in your love, that all the follies of this world and of each other will not have the power to separate you.

This day you will marry your friend, the one you laugh with, live for, dream with and love. As your marriage brings new meaning to love, so your love will bring new meaning to life. From this day forward let it be one promise, one dream, and one love.

Questions of consent

Will you take this person to be your partner/wife/husband/ your choice? Will you journey beside him/her from this day on? Will his/hers be the hand you hold, the heart you adore, the soul you honour and will you give him/her the freedom and the security within which he/she can thrive and flourish.

I will.

Or:

Will you take care of your partner's/wife's/husband's/your choice's life and his/her destiny? Will you value the gift of his/her love and his/her commitment to you? Will you always be mindful of the great responsibility you assume today for his/her well-being and will you always tend to him/her as to no other.

I will.

Or:

Will you love your partner/wife/husband/your choice unconditionally, whatever life may bring. Will you sleep beside him/her, walk beside him/her, laugh with him/her and cry with him/her? Will you love him/her with tenderness and with truth and take care to guard this precious love you share? Will you be there for him/her at the turning of the road and the rising of the path? Will you be his/hers from this day to the setting of your lives?

I will.

Question to each parent or guardian or asked collectively

You brought your child into the world. Through the tender years, you nursed them, loved them and watched over them. Your heart and your home has been their nourishment and as so often in the past he/she looks today for your favour. Do you offer your son/your daughter your blessing for their marriage?

I do.

Question to the guests

Will you, their friends and their family support them and be there for them in the days to come. Will you be generous in your care, thoughtful in your concern and imaginative in your friendship?

We will.

Introduction to the Vows

I invite you now to join your hands as you exchange your vows. The hand offered by each of you is a part of yourself. Cherish the touch for you touch not only your own life, but also that of another precious person. Be ever sensitive to your beloved, to their hopes and their dreams, and through the quality of your love, help make their dreams come true.

The Vows

Today I see you as if for the first time. For as much as I know you so well, you are new to me. Today you become my beloved partner in marriage. This is a beginning and a continuing; a whole new world and one that has already graced our lives.

Today, I give myself to you as your partner/wife/husband/your choice: all that I am, and all that I have; and I receive, the precious gift of you, as my beloved partner/wife/husband/your choice. For all the days of my life I will treasure you, I will cherish you and I will be utterly devoted to you, through the laughter and the tears, through the darkness and the light, I will be your everlasting love, your constant companion, your closest friend, pledging to you my deepest commitment. And this is my solemn vow.

Or:

Day by day I promise
To love and to honour you
To treasure you and to respect you
To walk with you side by side
In joy and sorrow
Day by day I promise
To hold you in my arms
To grow with you in truth
To laugh with you, to cry with you
To always be with you
And to love you with all that I am and all that I shall become
This I promise you from the depth of my heart, my mind and my soul,
For all our lives together.

Or:

From this day on I choose you, my beloved, to be my partner/wife/husband/your choice.
To live with you and laugh with you;
To stand by your side and sleep in your arms;
To be joy to your heart and food to your soul
To be your constant companion and closest friend;
To love you and bring out the best in you always;
And to be the best that I can be, for you.

Or:

To you I give my heart,
I give my soul,
I give my very self;
Into your hands I place
My hopes and dreams,
My strength and weakness.
To you I give my trust, my highest
And my best.
To you and only you will I be forever true.

Or:

No one has touched my life like you.
No one can compare with you,
No one has made my heart leap and my soul dance,
Nor set my mind alight with joy like you.
In your presence I have found my rest, my home and my self.
In your arms I have known such peace.
Today I give myself to you.
I am yours and ever shall it be.
Or:
On this momentous day,
It is my choice, my will and my delight,
To wed you my beloved.
Our love has changed my life; no more the search.
I have found you, my heart's desire,
And nothing will ever take me from your side,
You are my all and my only,
And with you shall I travel to my rest.
Or:
I want to spend the rest of my life with you.
I want to fall asleep each night with you by my side.
I want to tell you what fills my heart and my soul.
I want to love you forever and for always.
I want you to be the father/mother of my child.
I want you to be my lifelong friend and lover.
I want you to awaken my life with your love.
I want us to fill the coming years with wonderful memories.
I want us to face everything together.
I want you. I want you and me. I want us.
Or:
I love you
I love you unconditionally
I will love you whatever tomorrow brings
I will love you however much you change
My love is like a rock upon which you can build your life

My love is constant, certain and committed
My love will never waver, nor run dry
I declare that my lifelong vow
Is to so love you, day-by-day and year-by-year
That I become your greatest blessing,
And your richest source of happiness.
Or:
You are so beautiful/handsome to me,
You are my life, my light, my hope and my joy.
You are my food, my drink, my music and my song,
You are my warmth, my shelter, my passion and my rest.
You are my world.
And I am yours.
Your friend, your lover and your soulmate.
So let the whole world hear and know
That I love you
And I vow that my love will bring you joy.

The Ring Vows

You have brought two rings as a sign of your marriage.

A circle is the symbol of the sun and the earth and the universe. It represents wholeness and peace and a love, which never ever ends.

In the turning of the earth and the cycle of the seasons, in the dance of sun, moon and stars, on the great wheel of life which knows of no end or even its beginning; so the circle of love encompasses all, promises all, gives birth to all and protects all.

Give the rings now, that they may always remind you of how much you are in love, this great day when you commit and entrust yourselves to each other for all eternity.

I give you this ring, as a sign of our marriage. May we be encircled by each other's love, always close to each other, always secure in each other's care.

Or:

Whenever you hold this ring, know that I shall always come home to you, and my heart will be brimming over with love for you.

Or:

This ring is a symbol of all that I am. Receive and treasure it as a pledge of the love I have for you; and wear it to protect you whenever we are apart. From this day forward we are as one.

Or:

I give you this ring: because I love you, because I always want to be with you, because I place my life in your hands, because I will hold you forever.

Or:

I give you this ring, as a sign that I have chosen you above all others to share life's journey.

Or:

I bind you to me,
As I to you.
Golden mantle of my love,
Shining symbol of my eternal devotion.

Or:

I claim you this day as my own.
Wear this emblem of our love with pride.
Let all who see it know,
That with you I shall for ever abide.

The Declaration of Marriage

Inasmuch as they have grown in knowledge and love for one another, and because they have agreed in their desire to go forward in their life together, seeking an even richer and deeper relationship, and because they have pledged to meet sorrow and joy as one family, it gives me great pleasure to now pronounce that they are married.

Or:

Here in our presence intimate words have been spoken,

dreams unfurled and hopes set free. It has been our privilege to hear, to bear witness and to share these timeless moments. A love born in times past has today known its blossoming and, therefore, it is my joyful task to now announce that they are married partners.

Or:

Here before us they have embarked upon a unique journey. Their love will take them beyond the borders, across unknown continents, to whole new worlds beyond; but today we are with them, beside them, loving them, wishing them their highest dreams, bidding them safely on their way; for now they are husband and wife/husband and husband/wife and wife/married partners/your choice.

Or:

Something remarkable has taken place.

Two lives, once separate, have been joined.

In the giving, and the promising, in the hoping and the pledging,

a new world has been born, a new horizon glimpsed, a new path found, a new course set. They are now husband and wife/husband and husband/wife and wife/married partners/your choice.

Or:

We have heard with our ears and seen with our eyes.

Our hearts have been moved and our spirits stirred.

We have been witnesses to an eternal pledge, a lifelong commitment and a timeless hope. Today in our presence, they have become husband and wife/husband and husband/wife and wife/married partners/your choice.

A candle-lighting ceremony

Your love burns today as a flame within your hearts.

So join now those burning hearts and light up a torch of love.

The couple light individual candles and with them light a

central larger candle

Guard well this flickering light of love, that burning bright through happy days and darkest nights, it may forever provide your warmth, your direction and your hope.

A sharing of wine ceremony

You have shared together the fruits of love and your times together have been blessed.

Drink now this rich wine, fruit of the earth, symbol of life, of creation, of passion and of love.

The couple sip wine from the same silver vessel.

May the power of love, as strong wine ever flow within your veins, and may the taste of the grape always remind you of this moment when your mouths, as your lives, were burning with the joy of each other.

A sharing of honey ceremony

You have tasted the sweetness of love, intense and profound. Refresh each other now with the touch of honey upon your lips.

The couple in turn collect a tiny amount of honey with a silver spoon from a silver vessel and give it to each other.

May the touch of your lips, as your lives, be delicate and sweet, and as a thousand bees upon a thousand flowers have gathered this rich nectar may the exercise of your love be as constant and as colourful all your days.

Blessing the couple

May you know such love together; may you be sunlight for each other's growth, strength for each other's weakness, care for each other's pain, laughter for each other's success and in the unfolding of your lives may you become each other's greatest blessing.

Or:

May you become the greatest friends, the tenderest lovers, the most devoted companions, the most attentive listeners, the happiest playmates and the securest of couples.

Or:

May nothing in all of creation ever separate you from each other. May you stand strong against the dangers of tomorrow and stand tall in facing the challenges ahead. May your hope and trust in one another never fail and if damaged or under threat, may you discover unlimited resources of patience and forgiveness. May you learn to cope with every emotion, and all situations; the darkness and the light, the terrors of hell and the fruits of paradise. May the years bear witness to your love, which having passed the test of time, may deliver you into the last days, your hearts entwined, older, wiser, and so much more in love than in these headier days of your beginning. To such a journey, such an adventure, such a voyage of discovery we your family and friends commend you this day in greatest joy.

Or:

Let not a day pass without you expressing your love, reaffirming your devotion, nourishing one another. You hold within your marriage all that is precious, all that is good; value it among all things most highly and know that it is your source of life and happiness, and may that happiness be abundant for all the years to come.

Thoughts and hopes

(Select some of the paragraphs)

We celebrate the love that brought them to this day. With love that deepens through many years, may they come to know its meaning and its mystery.

May your house be a place of happiness for all who enter it, a place for growing, and a place for laughter. When shadows and darkness fall within its rooms, may it still be a place of hope and strength for all who enter. May no person be alien to your compassion. May your family be the family of all humankind.

And may you be blessed with a lifetime of joy.

At this moment rich with meaning, hope and promise, May the love that has brought you together continue to grow and enrich your lives.

No marriage is perfect for no one is perfect. So may you have unrelenting patience to accept each other's faults and failings and to learn to forgive one another fully and freely.

Express your thoughts and emotions, speak openly and honestly, listen to, encourage and respect one another. Protect the love you share and strive to be a living example of the beautiful relationship that is possible between two people.

Or:

We hope only good things for you.
We dream only good things for you.
We pray only good things for you.
Walk peacefully.
Dance joyously.
Love passionately.
Kiss tenderly.
Live fully and so may it only be.

Or:

How we long for your happiness.
Treasure one another as life's greatest gift.
Cherish the days you share,
The warm moments of your waking and sleeping,
The grind and marvel of your years side by side.
The intoxicating liquor of love with its pain and its passion.
Its loving and its hating.
Cherish all this.
It is but for a tiny moment
Upon life's ever turning wheel.

Or:

Caress the day you found each other.
Worship the ground upon which you stood.

Hallowed is the place of your becoming,
Hallowed is your touch that turns all to good.
Embrace the seconds of your talking,
Exalt the moments that you share,
Awesome is the ease that leaves predicting,
Awesome is the grace that finds us bare.
Absolve the torment of your failings,
Sanctify the rare quest to forgive
Divine is the freedom that means releasing
Divine is the love you pledge to live.

Or:

Fear not the morrow; alone you are no more.
Held in another's care.
The world awaits your coming.
Your destiny is a mystery, mischievously hiding.
Discover well its secrets and may you be surprised
By the excellence of love
When you are afraid, turn to each other.
When life is cruel, find refuge in each other.
When your horizons are vast, forget not each other.
When your hearts are full, be generous with each other.
And when many years have passed, be glad;
For in remaining true to one another,
You will have journeyed to the well of happiness
In each other's soul.

Or:

Today you are in love. Tomorrow you must love.
Love that values the other and seeks only their best.
Love that understands frailty and failure and is eager to forgive.
Love that copes with strange habits and surprising idiosyncrasies.
Love that swallows hard and laughs generously
Love that protects by foregoing beguiling pleasures.

Love that knows the time to weep and the time to smile.

Love that knows the mystery and privilege of crossing from the boundary of self to the other through their open and trusting heart.

Love that knows how to walk with humble step amidst the treasures of your beloved's soul.

Final blessings

May love be your blessing. May happiness be the gift you give one another. May peace and contentment be your reward. May hope overflow from within you. And may the source of all tenderness and care, resource you and protect you through the journey of your days and of your years.

Or:

May the emotions of these moments be constant visitors to your hearts.

May the warmth, smiles and laughter of your guests be heard and felt across the coming years.

May the intense beauty of these hours last for your lifetime together.

And may you never forget the rich love that is yours today.

Concluding words

Now, as this ceremony closes, may love and laughter, hope and happiness fill the air and flow from heart to heart. May old friendships be strengthened and new friendships born and in the interweaving of your lives may love surround you on this your wedding day and for all your days to come.

Or:

A wedding is a remarkable and beautiful occasion. We have been touched, moved and inspired today. Words about love, promises made in love and the innocence of the couple's love; all these things have refreshed us, challenged us and reminded us that nothing can compare with love. So as we turn from this ceremony to the excitement of the reception to follow, may our words and our conversations be full of love to bless the couple on this their marriage day.

Or:

The wedding is not over, it has just begun. Not once and forever, but again and again, shall the mystery of two people, together and in love, move them, and us, and touch the world. For marriage is not something said and done, but a promise whose fulfilment will grace the years ahead.

Or:

A symphony of words draws to its end. The *la*st strains of love's orchestra fill the air. Love is all around us and so it should be on this most profound of days. The wedding feast bids us welcome. Fine food and wine will carry us away to yet more happy hours and so let us with radiant smiles and happiest hearts greet the married couple.

Or:

The wedding service is almost over. It only leaves me to wish the married couple so much love and happiness for today and for a lifetime and to ask you all to make this the most unforgettable and wonderful day of their lives as you join them in celebrating their love, their hopes and their marriage.

Chapter 30

Words for the Thanksgiving of the Birth of a Child

(Personal names are inserted)

May peace and love and happiness be with you all today and always.

To the parent/s

This beautiful child you have brought for naming and blessing depends chiefly on you for the help and the encouragement s/he needs. Are you willing to give it to her/him by your example?

We are willing.

To the child

May your life be filled with love. May your days be filled with happiness. May no darkness eclipse your light. May you grow secure and confident, surrounded by the love of your family and your friends.

To the parent/s

You have the beautiful and challenging responsibility of guiding your child in the paths of goodness and light. Is it your desire and hope to bring your daughter/son up to resist those things that are harmful, to cleave to all that is good and to live a wholesome and productive life?

It is.

To the special people

You have been chosen by the family to bear a special responsibility of care and thoughtfulness towards this child. Through your friendship and example s/he will be nourished and blessed.

Is it your desire to fulfil this role now and for all your days?

It is.

Do you promise to encourage this child to fulfil her/his dreams and ambitions and to offer your guidance and support when it is needed?

We promise.

Do you promise to be there when s/he needs you, to offer your help, love, wisdom, friendship and understanding to her/him whenever you can?

We promise.

Do you promise to keep her/him safe from harm and keep her/him in your thoughts?

We promise.

Do you promise to support her/his parents in her/his upbringing whenever your help and assistance are needed?

We promise.

Then everyone gathers around the child and their parents into a circle and rainbow colours are woven around them.

Every rainbow is a reminder that love spreads colours across our lives through rain and sunshine. Whether you face storms, tempests or clement skies of blue, love will bear you safe.

We anoint you with the oil of blessing, gift from the stars.

Those invited dip their thumb/finger into some olive oil and touch the child's head/hair gently with it, making if they wish a shape/symbol, like a circle or rainbow or the first letter of the child's name.

We cleanse you with the waters of life; crystal streams promising light and hope.

A designated person pours water into a crystal bowl, letting it splash and encourages the child to touch the water with their fingers and play with it with their hands. As they do so the designated person sprinkles the child lightly and imperceptibly with a few tiny drops of water on their head/hair.

We encircle your life today with our love. Our hearts will

embrace you and our actions protect you.

Those invited kiss the child on the cheek.

We comfort you with the milk of love, flowing from the bosom of creation.

A designated person provides a drink of milk/bottle of milk or substitute, whatever is appropriate and either allows the child to drink it or just touches their lips with it.

As you receive abundant blessing and love, allow your life to issue forth beautiful energy and grace upon the earth and never be ashamed to stand up for what you believe to be right and good and to live your life in such a way that it will bring happiness and blessing to others and to yourself.

You have brought this beautiful child to be named. She/he is cherished in this circle of love.

What are the names that you have chosen for your daughter/son?

Will you love her/him and care for her/him; will you always accept her/him and seek to understand her/him; will you always be there for her/him through the twists and turns of her/his life, helping and supporting her/him through the dark places and laughing with her/him in the light; will you give her/his mind wings with which to fly and will you teach her/his heart to soar; will you lead her/him upon gentle paths and give her/him a love for truth and justice; will you cultivate in her/him a deep compassion for others and a respect for her/himself; will you show to her/him the beauty of this world and cover her/him in the sunlight of all that is good?

We will.

Then we name this child (her/his names are spoken by everyone). I inscribe her/his names upon the ground.

Here the designated person kneels and with her/his finger marks out the child's name upon the floor/grass/earth.

That this earth will provide a safe haven for her/his dwelling and her/his feet will find safe paths for her/his journeying.

We deliver her/him unto your earthly care.

The child is passed into the arms or care of the parent/s.

Tend her/him well for s/he is your child of love and there is nothing in all of creation that is more precious to you than your child/ren.

May you be blessed, May Love keep you and protect you. The sun will bring you light by day and the moon by night but may Love's light be forever bright within your heart and soul.

A candle is lit.

We give you this candle that you may shine as a light in the world and the light of our love will shine upon you, to warm you and to guide you. We are your friends and your family and we will always be here for you.

We hold her/him high to the heavens.

The parent/s lift the child up high.

We thank you from our hearts for the life of this child. Look after and protect her/him all her/his days to come and may s/he grow into a fine and good person bringing help and kindness to many. May her/his parents be blessed with ever deepening love, her/his home be filled with joy and peace and her/his future be bright and ever blessed.

Chapter 31

Words of Comfort for a Funeral

O gentle love
That brought us to birth
And into whose arms we die
In all our grief and pain, draw close and comfort us
Embrace us with your compassion
And fill our empty and aching hearts
With the promise of new life
That our loved ones are ever but a breath away.

* * *

We are hurting so much
We are so confused
Lost
Drowning in a sea of pain
We want to scream out – "Why!"
To understand
To turn the clock back
But we can't
We're helpless
We feel abandoned
And we cry out for help
May love come close
Amidst our tears and grieving
Hold us
Help us in our agony
And when it seems we can't cope
Can't face another day
Come lift us up

Carry us through this interminable darkness
This unbearable pain
Onto to the path of life and light and hope again.

* * *

Why do the clouds hang motionless above?
Why does my heart pause, its beat suspended?
Why does my chest tighten?
Tears fall…
It is for you my love
Why does the laughter drain from the earth?
Why does hope slip anxiously away?
Why do children fall silent at their play?
It is for you my love
And how do the trees stay still amidst the breeze?
And leaves, carousing, fall like lead…
And how does the sunlight cast shadows of the night?
Because you, my precious love, are dead.
And if this granite wall could but be broken
And if I knew how to vault upon the stars
And if I could in blinking, catch one moment more
Of your face, your touch, your life
Then true
This ache that gnaws my bones
My being
And my soul
Would not abate
But in that fleeting moment
We would know
That never
Til we meet again
Will you leave my side
My heart

My very self.

* * *

Was that a star that caught my eye?
Was that a leaf, that falling waved?
Was that a fox that howled for me?
Or was it you?
Was that a breeze that stroked my cheek?
Was that a wave that called?
Was that the moon that lit my face?
Or was it you?
My angel
My love and my life.
For whom I search
Endless nights and days
I have no more to give
My tears – the oceans
My weeping – the wind
And if it was you
Then
Steal quietly in
While I sleep
Dew, a kiss upon my face
That shining moist with daybreak's light
I may know
You near

* * *

Oh my beloved
How we have loved you
How you have loved us
Can it be that all these years have passed?

So many memories
Of your hopes and heartaches
Your gentle words and ways
That have interlaced our days
And now this sacred vessel of your spirit
Once so vibrant with life
Lies still and quiet
No heart to beat
No pulse to course
A body for which you have no further use
Around which we gather to have cremated (to be buried)
(Earth to earth)
Ashes to ashes
Dust to dust
But you are now free
Delivered to the wide blue expanse of the sky
To the sun's warmth
And the wind's breath
To the dance of the stars and the planets.
Go safely
Across the rainbow bridge
Of all our dreams and hopes
To the paradise beyond
Into the arms of loved ones
Waiting upon that golden shore
And oh how we will miss you
But until that great day of reunion
Our love will remain ever with **you**

* * *

We leave our beloved not here
He/she comes with us
To share all that lies ahead

We hold him/her close
As with all our loved ones, passed over
Forever safe within our hearts.
And as we travel on to the life that lies ahead
May we hold and comfort one another
Through these days of grief
Ourselves held in the palm of love's hand
Until that brighter tomorrow
When a new day dawns.

* * *

Part VIII

Chapter 32

95 Theses – Love in Action

In 1517 Martin Luther affixed to the door of the castle church at Wittenberg his 95 theses against indulgences. He became an active proponent of reform in the church and played a considerable role in the Reformation.

In 1999, aware of how the Church had lost its way again, I wrote 95 theses and nailed them to the door of Canterbury Cathedral where St Augustine had formed his first church in this country.

I did so in the hope that they would help point to a comprehensive reform required of the church.

Belief and believing has to be about love, governed by love, practiced in love, creating love and inspiring love.

The theses set out how love could be expressed in the Christian world.

I was arrested.

The cathedral authorities did not want me to put the theses on the door to Canterbury Cathedral, even though I tried to find a means of attaching them that would be acceptable to the authorities, even using blutack!

They invited the police to attend and I was arrested and taken to the police station, although the police expressed their regret at having to arrest me.

I was released on bail. A few weeks later I was told that I was not going to be charged with any offence.

The 95 Theses

1. 'God is love and those who live in love, live in God and God lives in them.'

   Jesus said, love your neighbour as yourself.

There are three things that last forever: faith hope and love
But the greatest of them is love.
The premise of the following theses is that the church has one supreme commission, which is to love.

2. Love is unconditional. It is grace, freely offered, freely given, freely received.
3. Love never rejects, condemns, excludes.
4. Love listens, learns and accommodates.
5. Love forgives and never reneges its responsibility to all.
6. Love is not willing to cast aside, alienate or ostracise. Love cherishes every life form.
7. Love is characterised by an open door, by possibility, opportunity and encouragement.
8. Anyone who loves is Christian in spirit.
9. Anyone who forgives is Christian in spirit.
10. All who serve others are Christian in spirit. It matters not whether they are from another faith or have no faith. Whether they live in a conventional manner or alternative. Wherever love is visible in actions, God is at work and the Christian spirit is manifest.
11. Love invites the church to seek out and serve all who so display the presence of God in their work and lives, the real Christians who may never choose to enter a church building.
12. Love invites the church to stop devoting its attention to the few who attend worship and to turn most of its attention instead to the vast numbers, who don't,
14. Love invites Christians to stop investing their time and attention in church pursuits within the church family and instead to be imaginative about and committed to expressing love to those outside the church family.
15. Love invites the church to cherish creation and all living creatures and to be at the forefront of campaigning to protect the world and environment.
16. Love invites the church to cherish every human being,

affording them respect and dignity and allowing for no discrimination on any ground whatsoever.

17. Love resists the rise in evangelicalism and fundamentalism in the church today. There is no neat systematic method of packaging God or faith. Love encourages variety not uniformity.

Rites

Baptism

18. It is not love that leads the church to reject many of those who ask to be baptised. No one was refused baptism In the Gospels. All who came were baptised.
19. It is not love that leads the church to require a priest to refuse baptism to a person from another parish, unless they have obtained their parish priest's permission first.
20. The church should always be willing to baptise anyone who asks to be baptised. There should be no requirements laid upon them, no conditions set and no obstacles put in their way. They should experience the grace of God in the open, warm, unconditional acceptance and granting of their request. This is love.
21. Love invites the clergy to offer ministry to everyone and anyone: Never to turn away an applicant for baptism, never to turn away applicants for marriage, always to invite everyone to communion, always to offer acceptance and respect and ministry whatever a person's beliefs or lifestyle.
22. It is not love that leads the church to refuse baptism to parents who are not married. The church has no divine authority to withhold the grace of God from any person, whatever their state or condition; whatever their approach to life or beliefs.

Communion

23. It is not love that leads the church to withhold from so many people the invitation to Jesus' table. There is no record that Jesus wanted this selective approach.
24. The church should always invite everyone to receive communion irrespective of whether they are confirmed, Christian or atheist. This is love.
25. It is not love that leads the church to corrupt the symbol of communion by administering it in an exclusive and divisive way.
26. It is not love that leads the church to bar children from receiving communion. How can the church share a family meal and exclude the most vulnerable and needy?
27. The church should invite babies and all children to receive communion. This is love.

Marriage

28. It is not love that leads the church to reject many people who ask to be married in church, if they have been divorced. Jesus warned us not to judge or condemn. Jesus showed us how to practice forgiveness and how to find the path of resurrection. How then can the church judge, withhold forgiveness and deny applicants for marriage the benefits of resurrection?
29. Love invites the church to marry anyone who asks to be married in church.
30. Love invites the church to marry gay, lesbian and trans-sexual couples in church, as well as those who live in an alternative or unconventional way.

Worship

31. Love invites the clergy to stop exercising control over the expression *of* people's spirituality. Lay people should be encouraged to take services, including communion and

baptism. Experiments in worship and in different ways of believing should be encouraged.

Equal Opportunities

Discrimination According to Gender

32. It is not love that leads the church to be institutionally sexist.
33. Love invites the church to operate an equal opportunities policy, ensuring that both men and women are equally represented at every level of church life. Reactionary and prejudiced views can't be allowed to find refuge behind the guise of theology or principles of faith. Love would afford to everyone equal rights, responsibilities, status and respect.
34. Love invites women bishops to be appointed without delay.

Discrimination According to Race

35. It is not love that leads the church to be institutionally racist.
36. Love invites the church to operate an equal opportunities policy ensuring that all the races represented within this land have equal access to every level of church life. At present the selection process discriminates against those from ethnic minorities. Love would seek out and include all and everyone.

Discrimination According to Ability

37. It is not love that leads the church to discriminate against the disabled.
38. Love is offended that the majority of churches have no or inadequate facilities for the disabled. The church regards the provision of such facilities as a low priority. Love invites every church at once to install toilet facilities and proper access for the disabled to and within the building.
39. Love invites the church to install Braille books and loop amplification systems in all churches

40. It is not love that leads the church to discriminate against the disabled by preventing them from becoming priests. Love invites the church to provide resources, both human and financial, to overcome this.

Discrimination According to Lifestyle

41. It is not love that leads the church to discriminate against those who adopt alternative lifestyles.
42. It is not love that has led the church to become a place hijacked by the respectable and conventional. Those who live differently feel ostracised and abandoned by the church. The church is for everyone.
43. Love invites the church to cease its judgemental commentary about people's lives and aspire to become the place of absolute and unconditional acceptance and love.
44. It is not love that leads the church to interfere in the expression of love in people's relationships.
45. Love finds the Pope's teaching about contraception and the prohibition of Roman Catholic clergy from marrying an abhorrence. Love finds the Anglican requirement that sex should only take place within marriage an abhorrence. Love finds the teaching of the church that homosexuals and homosexual priests refrain from the physical expression of their sexuality an abhorrence.
46. Love invites the church to stop playing God and to stop issuing dictates that are scientifically flawed and morally questionable.
47. It is not love that leads the church to be characterised as rejecting, judging, condemning and saying NO. The church places burdens of guilt and self-recrimination upon people's backs and does so little to release them or heal them.
48. The church should rise to the requirement to be at the forefront of innovative and enlightened thinking, keeping pace with a modern world and thinking anew theologically

and ethically.

49. In the twenty-first century, it is likely that unimaginable scientific advances will be made. Correspondingly, the church must be ready to advance its own insights.
50. History and increased knowledge have exposed the subjective nature of much so-called truth. The church must, therefore, display a humility and flexibility when pronouncing on moral issues.

Discrimination According to Age

51. It is not love that leads the church to be unfriendly places for children. Love invites the church to clear play areas within the church for children, as well as providing crèche, nappy-changing and bottle-warming facilities. Children should also be welcome at and fully involved in services, including leading them.

Discrimination According to Culture

52. It is not love that leads the church to be culturally elitist, services and church life generally display a distinct ecclesiastical culture, which has to be learnt and often poses a barrier to people becoming involved.
53. Love invites the church to relax the control it exercises through Canon law and permit widespread parochial experimentation both in worship and church decision-making and to encourage the local church to reflect the culture and traditions of the people.

Theology

54. Love cannot take the church seriously if it is unwilling or incapable of reforming its theological teaching.
55. It is not love that leads the church hierarchy to deceive the congregations by withholding the insights of modern theology and research.

56. It is not love that leads the church to expect Christians to believe the bible stories in a simplistic and literal way.
57. It is not love that leads the church to resist proper enquiry by confusing the enquirer with complex and often nonsensical dogma.
58. Love knows that the origins of all church teaching and dogma are simple and clearly understood truths. It is not love that has led the church to conceal those truths and often to destroy them in the development of ever more complicated theological teaching.
59. It is not love that has lead the church to distort Jesus' simple meal of love and his simple symbolic gestures into devilish arguments about flesh and blood and who can and can't receive. The church has harvested only blood and bitterness by so doing and still does.
60. It is not love that has lead the church to deny people full access to God by describing God in Trinitarian language that no bishop or theologian has ever been able to explain adequately to the people.
61. It is not love that that has led to church teaching enshrining and perpetuating prejudice, and because the church claims such teaching is absolute has allowed it to act as a moral cancer in the development of ethics.
62. The language of the Trinity presents God as Father and Son and Holy Spirit. It is not love that leads the church to describe God in language which originated in ancient philosophy and which appears patriarchal, gender biased and nonsensical in today's world.
63. It is not love which leads the church to continue such bias in referring to Jesus as the ' Son of God` while failing to name another the 'Daughter of God'.
64. It is not love that leads the church to mislead people by teaching that Jesus was perfect and sinless when even the Bible shows otherwise. It is not love that the church requires

people to follow the example of this so-called perfect Jesus and so debilitates them with guilt at their own failure to do so, which makes them dependent on the church for forgiveness.

65. It is not love that obscures the truth that Jesus was a man like any other, a mixture of good and bad, whose genius was to learn how to integrate his life for the benefit of others in the practice of love.
66. It is not love that leads the church to mislead the people by teaching that the words of the Bible are all God's words instead of encouraging them to read the Bible critically, discarding the bad and cherishing the good.
67. It is not love that leads the church to teach about hell and judgement as realities after death, when love could never treat their own child in such a way.
68. It is not love that leads the church to teach that Christianity is the one, true and only way to God and that all other faiths are inferior.
69. It is not love that leads the denominations to be divided, to reject each other's ministers and priests and to bar each other's worshippers from receiving communion.
70. Love invites the church to stop trying to impose dogma onto people and instead to preach the simple truth of love.
71. Love invites the church to teach that describing Jesus as the son of God is to make the point that all of us are God's children, sons and daughters of God and need to live our lives and treat each other, accordingly.
72. Love invites the church to teach that describing Jesus as having a bodily resurrection is to make the point that all of us can endure suffering and be restored.
73. Love invites the church, rather than describing God in Trinitarian language, to describe God as the God of love, who loves everyone, who loves everything, who invites us to love everyone and everything too.

74. Love invites the church to teach that describing the supernatural, the miracle stories and the extraordinary is to make the point that through living life to the full we can make our lives extra ordinary, super natural and miraculous.
75. Love invites the church to teach that instead of it being essential to take Holy Communion each week, all of us in our everyday lives should sit down to eat with friends and enemies alike.

Organisation

76. Love rebukes the church for putting philosophy, power and politics before the central commission to love.
77. It is not love that leads the church to operate like a massive business empire. The church spends vast amounts of money maintaining buildings, paying for administrative structures, and supporting the lavish lifestyles of many of its employees.
78. The churches and cathedrals are the heritage of the British people and yet those very people are increasingly denied access to them, the church exercises tight controls, with times of entry and entry charges and limitations as to who may use the building.
79. Love invites the church to divest itself of all its buildings. The spirit does not exist in bricks and mortar. Worship cannot be confined to sanctuary or chancel, it begs release.
80. Love invites the church to divest itself of its responsibilities for church buildings and cathedrals. All such properties could be made over to and held in trust by the trustees of a newly formed charity, a Trust, like the National Trust, perhaps named The Ecclesiastical Trust.
81. The Ecclesiastical Trust could then maintain the buildings independently.
82. Love invites churches and cathedrals, administered under these reforms by the Ecclesiastical Trust, to be made

available to everyone to offer worship and other appropriate events and for clergy to be willing to take services in them for everyone.

83. Love invites the church to sell all bishops' residences and vicarages and leave all clergy to be responsible for arranging their own accommodation.
84. It is not love that decides that the church commissioners and many church officials are paid high salaries and that bishops and archdeacons are paid higher amounts than vicars. Love invites all clergy and church officials to receive the same income.
85. It is not love that has arranged for bishops to live in palaces and most vicars to reside in larger houses than their parishioners. It is not love that arranges for bishops to ride in chauffeur-driven cars and be regular guests at royal and political dinners for the wealthy.
86. It is not love that determines that the majority of a bishop's time is spent mixing with the articulate and the powerful, is spent with clergy and church officials, is spent in meetings and conferences, is spent with the few who go to church.
87. Where are the bishops and priests who spend the majority of their time expressing love to the poor, the powerless, the persecuted, the homeless and the abandoned in society? Where are the bishops and priests who spend the majority of their time expressing love by giving time to the weak, by dining with the beggars and by rubbing shoulders daily with the downcast? Love invites the clergy to surrender their stipend and to live from their own endeavour.
88. It is not love that guides the church to use its vast reserves of wealth to pay for its own infrastructure and to benefit its own clients, as any business or company would do, but only gives a minute proportion to the poor and to those outside the church.
89. Love invites the church to become poor, by withdrawing its

investments and selling its assets and using them solely for the physical and psychological well-being of the people of this country and of the world.

In Conclusion

90. Love is willing to admit mistakes, recognise that certain traditions, teachings and rules are flawed and progress to a more enlightened understanding and practice. The church of the twenty-first century needs radical reform making it unrecognisable from what now exists.
91. Love invites worship to be woven into the everyday fabric of life, taking place in homes, gardens, pubs, nightclubs, sports centres, beauty spots, hotels; everywhere and anywhere.
92. Love invites the bishops and priests to be released from their preoccupations with buildings, synods and committees, politics and prestige. Love invites them back onto the road, a mobile resource visiting and ministering to the people of this country, whatever their beliefs or ways.
93. Love invites the clergy to speak about God simply and to identify God in everyday loving forms of behaviour and to encourage people to greater expressions of love in their lives.
94. Love invites the clergy to live and to encourage Christians to live their beliefs in practice rather than in ritual; action as prayer, eating with the poor as communion, reconciliation as repentance.
95. If the Church of England, the Catholic Church and all other denominational churches are to survive in the next century, it will *only* be through a reformation as comprehensive as any hitherto. In order to be so reformed it is necessary for what is, to die and be reborn through love. It is my earnest prayer and hope that this will happen for the sake of this generation and all that are to come.

CHRISTIAN
ALTERNATIVE

Throughout the two thousand years of Christian tradition there have been, and still are, groups and individuals that exist in the margins and upon the edge of faith. But in Christianity's contrapuntal history it has often been these outcasts and pioneers that have forged contemporary orthodoxy out of former radicalism as belief evolves to engage with and encompass the ever-changing social and scientific realities. Real faith lies not in the comfortable certainties of the Orthodox, but somewhere in a half-glimpsed hinterland on the dirt track to Emmaus, where the Death of God meets the Resurrection, where the supernatural Christ meets the historical Jesus, and where the revolution liberates both the oppressed and the oppressors.

Welcome to Christian Alternative... a space at the edge where the light shines through.